IMAGES
of Modern America

AMESBURY

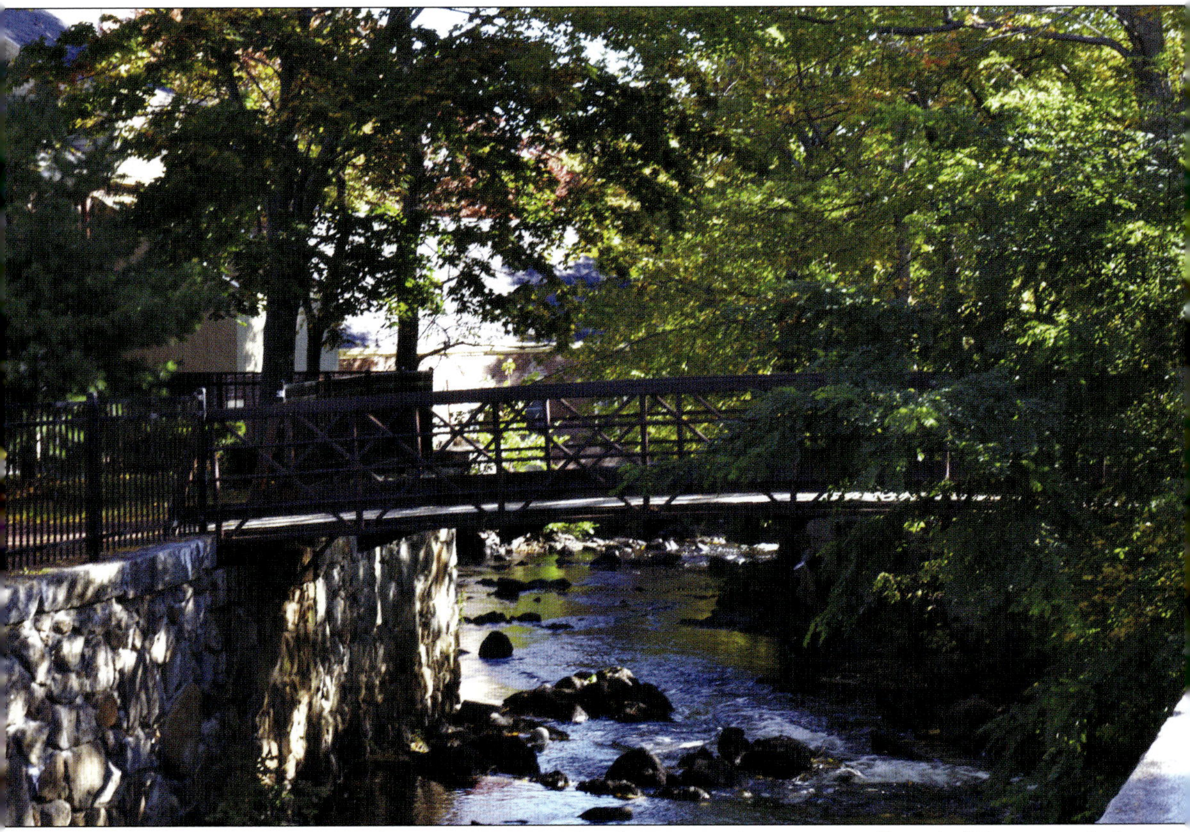

This bridge runs over the Powow River leading into the upper millyard. (Photograph by the author.)

On the Front Cover: Clockwise from top left:
Ice boats on Lake Attitash (Photograph by Betty Goodwin; courtesy of the Amesbury Public Library; see page 36), Earl Young, Charlotte Young, Esther Burke, Irene Wilson, Frances Brown, and Betty and Ernestine Goodwin (Courtesy of the Amesbury Public Library; see page 64), Amesbury High School majorettes and band (Courtesy of the Amesbury Public Library; see page 45), Amesbury Public Library's 100th anniversary (Photograph by the author; see page 62), Coastal Connections: (first row) Jay Chipman, Ben Bunnell, and Frances Darbyshire; (second row) Sheila Skane (CFO) and Deb Plumer (executive director); (third row) Nathan Pouliot, Alexa Watt, and Craig Powers (Photograph by Joey Walker; see page 10)

On the Back Cover: From left to right:
Camp Bauercrest (Courtesy of Camp Bauercrest; see page 42), Fireball Run (Photograph by the author; see page 82) Ava Garvey (Photograph by Joey Walker; see page 53)

IMAGES
of Modern America

AMESBURY

Margie Walker

ARCADIA
PUBLISHING

ISBN 978-1-4671-3416-3

Published by Arcadia Publishing
Charleston, South Carolina

Printed in the United States of America

Library of Congress Control Number: 2015941219

For all general information, please contact Arcadia Publishing:
Telephone 843-853-2070
Fax 843-853-0044
E-mail sales@arcadiapublishing.com
For customer service and orders:
Toll-Free 1-888-313-2665

Visit us on the Internet at www.arcadiapublishing.com

This book is dedicated to my husband, Joey Walker, my parents, Natalie and Roy Shepard, Margie and Jack Hart, and in memory of Dottie Therrien. I want to thank all of the people of Amesbury both past and present that continue to help build a strong community.

Contents

Acknowledgments

The Amesbury Public Library with their vast collection of local history materials was an enormous resource for this book. Thank you to the Amesbury residents as well as people throughout the United States that came forward with stories, photographs, and information. I would like to thank the Amesbury Fire Department, Steve Allen, Amesbury Carriage Museum, Joni Baptiste, Wayne Barbaro, James Bateman, Peter Bryant, Alan Bull, Kathy Colby, Todd Calderwood, Dianne Cole, Suzanne Cote, Bonnie and Gary Crocker, Peg Cronin, Ronald Gagnon, Steve Deorocki, Jennifer Freeman, Julie Gilchrist, Jeff Gilchrist, Betty Goodwin, Tom Hanshaw, Rhonda and David Hodge, Steve Holbrook, Peter Hoyt, Kathy Jordan, RJ Knecht, James Kukene, Blake Lemke, Wayne Louth, Karen MacTavish, Doug, Matthew, Colin and Rose McBride, Melissa McElaney, Iain McGregor, Carol Metcalf, Jim Nolan, Paula Noon, Bob Pare, Normand Pare, Jeff Picard, Justin Petrillo, Deb Plumer, Eric Rightor, Robert Serino for letting us use your truck, Taylor Simpson, Sheila Skane, Michelle Stanton, Mike Sweeney, Anne Tunstall, Marie Veilleux, Janet Wetherbee, Thomas White, and Sheila Zindroski. A special thank-you goes to my husband, Joey, for supporting everything that I do, pushing me when I needed it, keeping me on track, and taking all the photographs that I needed. I want to thank everyone that contributed to this book.

INTRODUCTION

Amesbury was incorporated in 1668. Amesbury was known for carriage-making, the automobile industry, peanut butter, and other industries. In the 1960s, LeBaron Bonney was making upholstery for vintage cars, Myron Cowden was building boats along the Merrimack River, and Dennis "Ski" Iworsky was off to Vietnam. The Colby family came home for a reunion, and the Bartlett Museum opened. The oldest house in Amesbury, the Osgood house, was dismantled and moved to Dover, Massachusetts.

People were skiing at Locke's Ski Hill and swimming, kayaking, and canoeing at Lake Attitash, Lake Gardner, and Tuxbury Pond. You could navigate the trail at Battis Farm, walk along the Powow River at the Riverwalk, or explore Woodsom Farm. The Kimballs were making jellies and jams, Norman's was the place to go for a good meal, you could buy clothes at Evangeline's, and the Starbirds were selling and repairing jewelry. Amesbury High School burned in 1964, and a 1917 time capsule was discovered. Students were in plays and on television shows and participating in the Amesbury Public Library Summer Reading Program. In 1992, some 400 volunteers came out to help build a playground at the town park in memory of Bertha Shattler Ashby of Virginia.

In 1996, the Town of Amesbury became the City of Amesbury. September 11, 2001, was devastation that we never imagined possible. We were shell-shocked and not able to comprehend what had happened. Now, 14 years later, we are still grieving for the loss of life that happened on that day and wondering why. None of the people lost that day and their families will ever be forgotten. We have remembrances every September 11 in which police, firefighters, local politicians, and people of the community come together and remember. The Amesbury Public Library celebrated its 100th anniversary, and Relay for Life began to bring awareness to the citizens of Amesbury in 2002 of the dangers of cancer. Amesbury Days is still going strong 116 years later, with the same mission as the first year. It is 10 days of events that bring different activities and entertainment to Amesbury, ending with fireworks at Woodsom Farm on the Fourth of July. Memorial and Veterans Day remembrances are held every year to remember the men and women that have fought for our freedom. On Memorial Day, veterans go to each of the cemeteries and place wreaths on the graves. They also go to Alliance Park, where they throw a wreath into the Merrimack River for the men and women lost at sea. A parade is held and then a ceremony at Landry Stadium. In May 2014, the doughboy that stands in front of Amesbury Middle School was restored and rededicated to a huge crowd. The statue of the World War I soldier and the accompanying veterans' memorial were originally dedicated in 1929. Frances Justin was seven years old when the doughboy was first dedicated and attended the rededication in 2014.

Time capsules from 1874 and 1917 were found and opened with anticipation of what would be inside. In the 1874 time capsule, the names of the Civil War soldiers from Amesbury were listed. These men wanted to be remembered, and they were. In the 1917 time capsule, town reports, photographs, and school materials were found. It is amazing that after all of the years the materials were still in excellent condition.

When the Boston Marathon bombing happened, we pulled together and held a vigil to show support for the victims and their families. The community gathered at the gazebo and came together. Our middle school students and members of the community sent their hearts to the residents and families of Sandy Hook Elementary School in Connecticut. Our community does not only care about what happens in Amesbury but also what happens in other parts of the country.

Amesbury has many churches in town, all of which have been here since the 1800s. They are providing services for people of all ages with food pantries, thrift shops, prayer groups, child care, and other services. The first Saturday of November, Amesbury celebrates the Village of Church Fairs. All of the churches have their Christmas fairs on the same day. The city comes alive with excitement as people go from church to church to find those special treasures. Lunch is served at all of the churches, each with their own specialty.

The 300th anniversary of Amesbury and the bicentennial were major events. Representatives from Amesbury, England, came bringing gifts. Residents contributed their family recipes to create a cookbook, coins were manufactured, and people dressed in period costume and walked the streets of Amesbury. The bicentennial had the militia, parades, dances, plays, and other events. Josiah Bartlett, an Amesbury resident, signed the Declaration of Independence. People of all ages came out in their period dress. Events were held at the training field on Monroe Street, where George Washington addressed the troops. Children raised the Union flag, and Amesbury was transported back in time. A lot of time went into these events. All of the volunteers that helped with these celebrations deserve a huge thank-you.

Amesbury is all about tradition, family, and community. When a neighbor is in need, the community rallies and helps support them. As you will see in the photographs, there are many events that the community is involved in. Events are for all ages; from the youngest to the oldest everyone has a good time. People are involved in this community and passionate about the direction that we go in. The upper millyard is complete. In 2015, they started the revitalization of the lower millyard with the Amesbury Carriage Museum, the chamber of commerce, and a visitor's center being the focal point of the project. Heritage Park will be built along the Powow River—a nice addition.

Many leave Amesbury and go to other places to live and work, but they all have one thing in common—they can all call Amesbury home.

One

Business

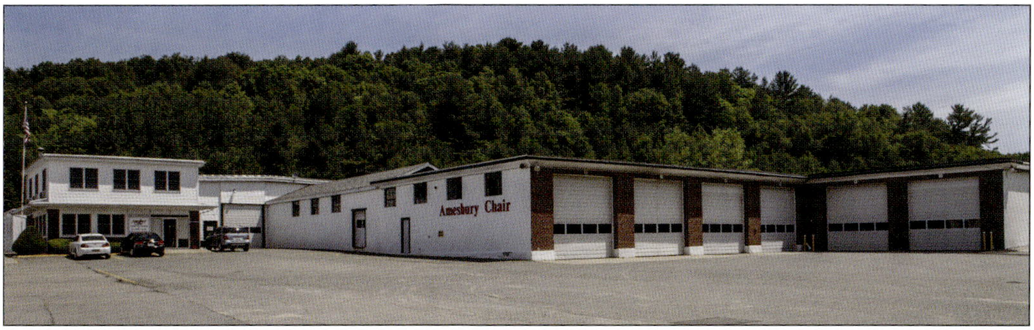

R&G Manufacturing Company was founded in 1948 by Sal and John Barbaro. Producing iceboxes, the company began making metal kitchen and storage cabinets. During the 1960s, it expanded to include wooden dinette sets under the Amesbury Chair name. Making its own furniture, the company distributed wooden chairs, tables, and rockers throughout New England. In their 67th year of business, they sell dining and bedroom furniture through stores and the Amesbury Furniture Outlet. They are proud of their Amesbury roots and the Barbaro family legacy. (Photograph by Joey Walker; courtesy of Wayne Barbaro.)

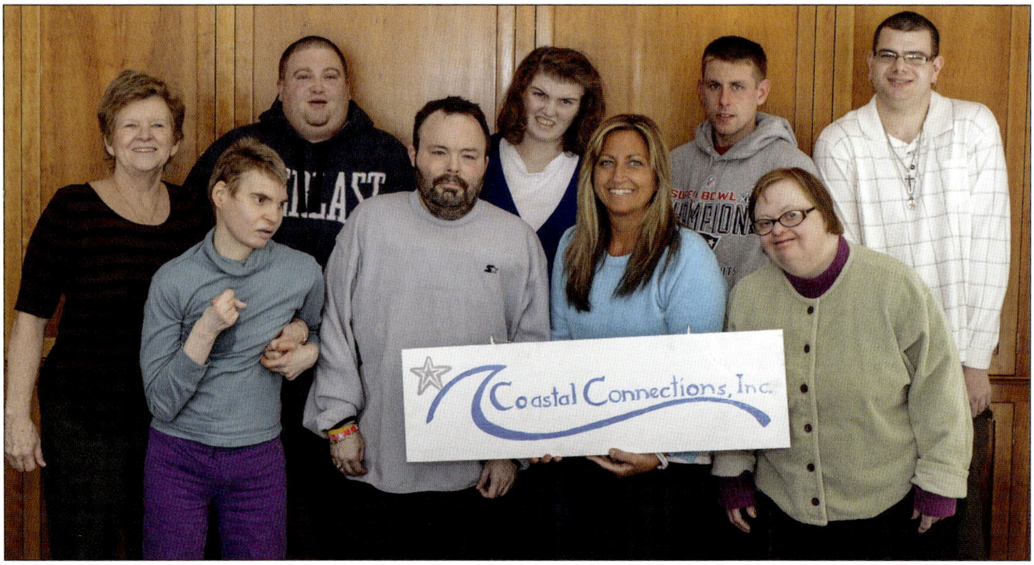

Coastal Connections opened in Amesbury in January 2010, with Deborah Plumer as the executive director. The people attending Coastal Connections quickly became a part of Amesbury's culture. It is a program for adults with disabilities to make a difference in their own lives and a difference in the community. They were embraced by the city by joining forces with other community organizations and businesses. They work with Flatbread, setting tables and making boxes; are models for students at the Cosmetology Program at Whittier Vocational High School; give tours to students at the Whittier Home; work at their own thrift shop; recycle materials; and offer art for sale at a consignment shop in town. They learn social, communication, and sensory-motor skills; practice independent living; and perform community service. (Both, photograph by Joey Walker.)

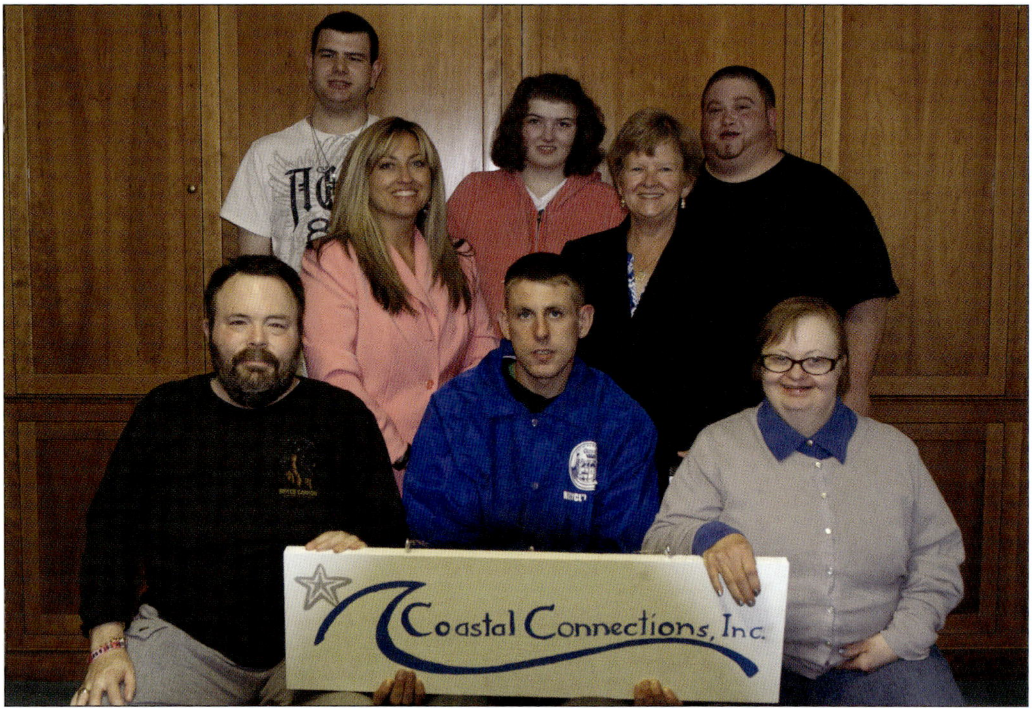

Wally Jardis opened Amesbury Industrial, located in the old Strand Theater, in 1973. Jardis purchased the business from Frank Cynewski. In 1976, his son Greg Jardis (pictured at right) took over the business. In 1983, Greg bought the old Bailey No. 2 Mill building on High Street, which is shown in the 2015 photograph below. Greg supplies the store with over 60,000 American-made products. Some of his employees have been working there for over 35 years. Greg was involved with the upper millyard project since its inception. He feels that the community has been very good to him and desires to give back as much as he can. He donated space to Our Neighbors' Table so that they can continue to offer meals to people that are struggling. Amesbury Industrial is not just a hardware store. It is a community-based business with loyal customers where everyone is made to feel like family. (Both, photograph by Joey Walker; courtesy of Greg Jardis.)

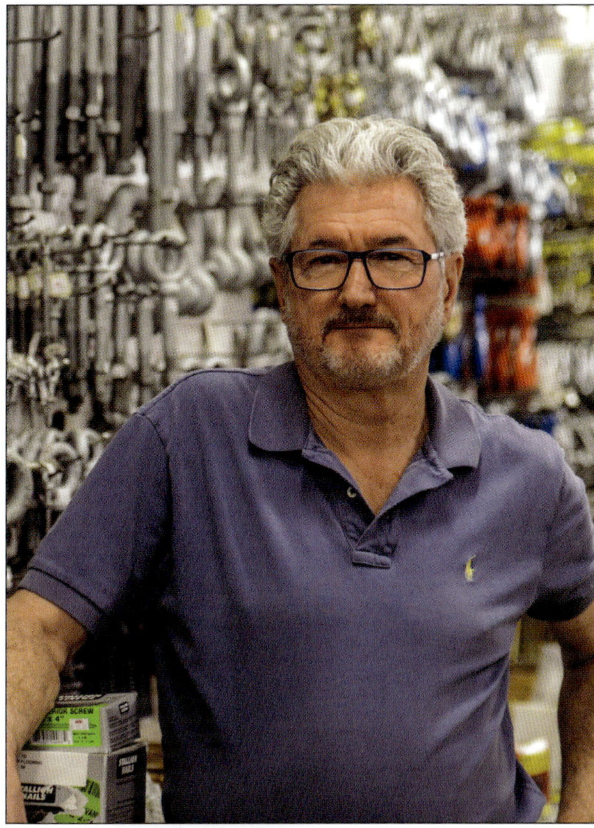

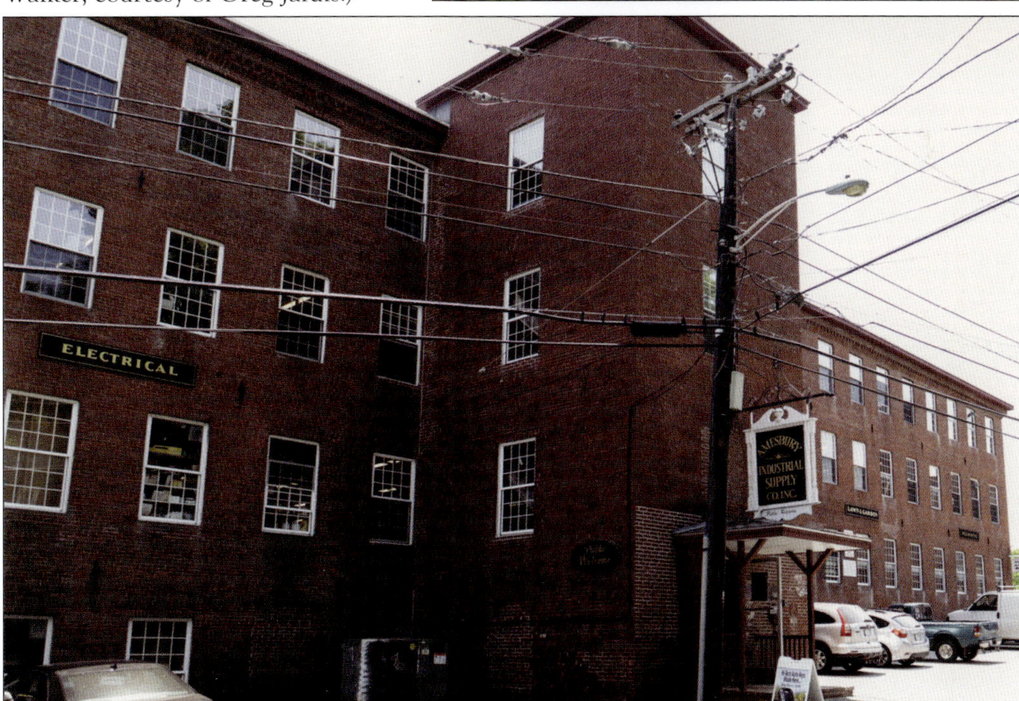

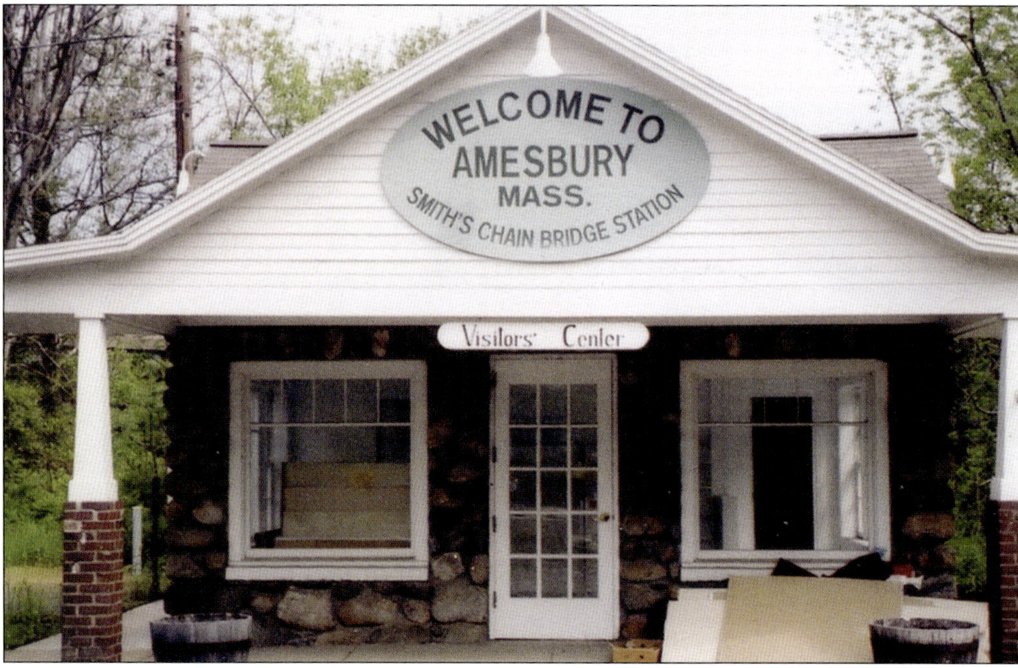

Smith's Chain Bridge Filling Station was built in 1930. It was a filling station until 1970. It was then converted into a car wash. It closed in 1986. Around 1997, a grant was obtained to preserve the station. The Amesbury Improvement Association planted trees. The station opened as a Visitor Center in 1999. Volunteers answered tourists' questions and gave directions to points of interest. (Courtesy of the Amesbury Public Library.)

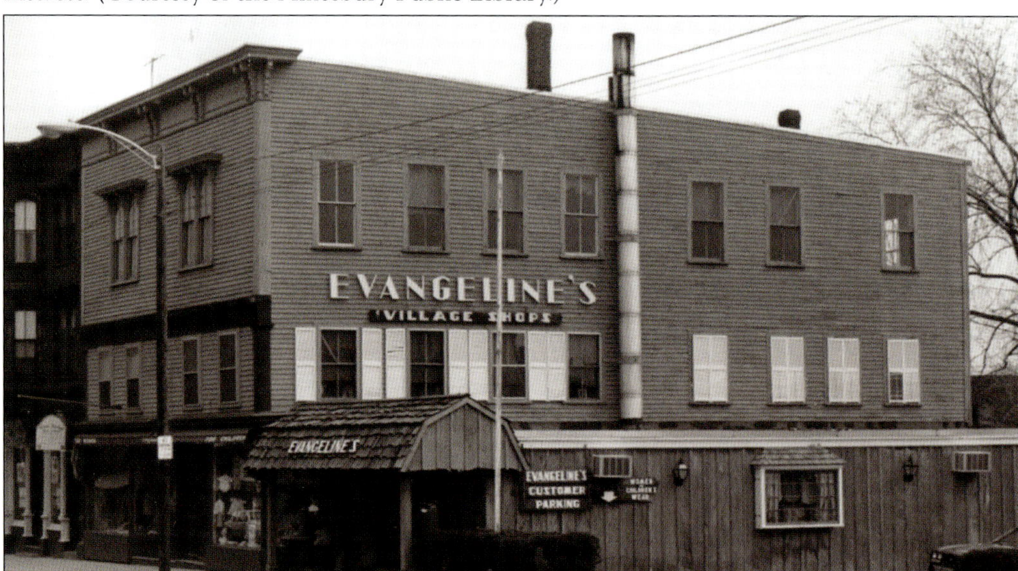

Evangeline's was a mainstay on Main Street for over 50 years. Francis Hession and his wife, Evangeline, were the youngest merchants in Amesbury when the store opened in 1936. At Evangeline's, one could buy clothes for women and children. Much of the success of the business was the long-term employees; there were four mother-and-daughter teams. (Courtesy of the Amesbury Public Library.)

Richard and Ruth Kimball (pictured here) started the R.E. Kimball Company in 1955, selling high-quality wholesale jams and jellies to businesses. Richard passed in 1994, and their daughter Joy Kimball took over the business. Ruth passed away in 2001. When Joy's daughters Kim and Kate graduated from college, they joined the company, making Kimball's a third-generation business. They use Grade A fruits and vegetables and never any artificial flavors or preservatives—everything is 100 percent natural. They only have one 75-gallon kettle; every batch is made in it. Every product is made by hand, using no automated machinery. They have expanded the line and now have close to 130 flavors. They still keep the same quality standards that Richard and Ruth imposed, and they always will. Kimball's products can be found throughout New England. (Both, courtesy of Kate Gilbert, Kim Owen, and Joy Kimball.)

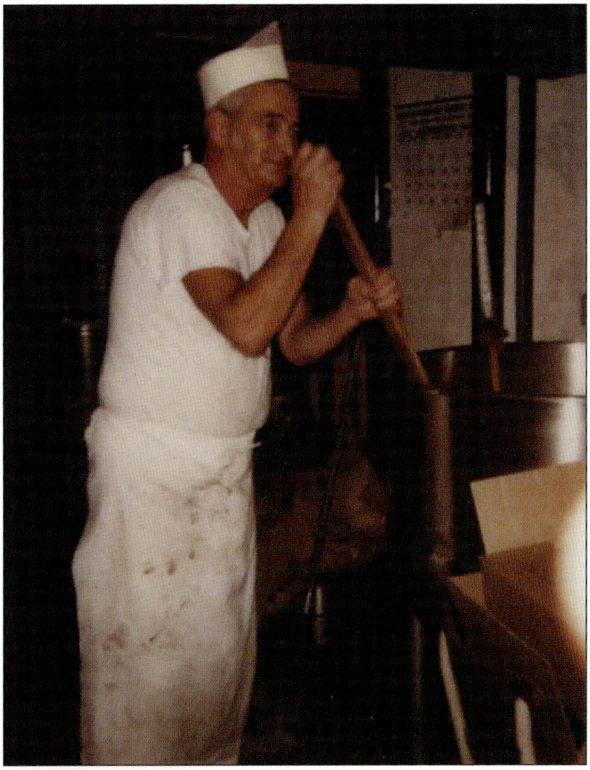

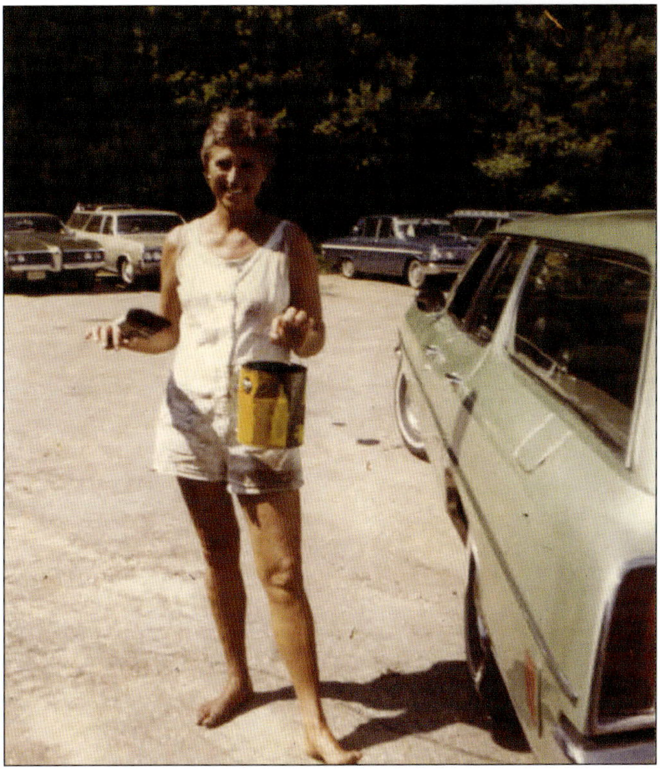

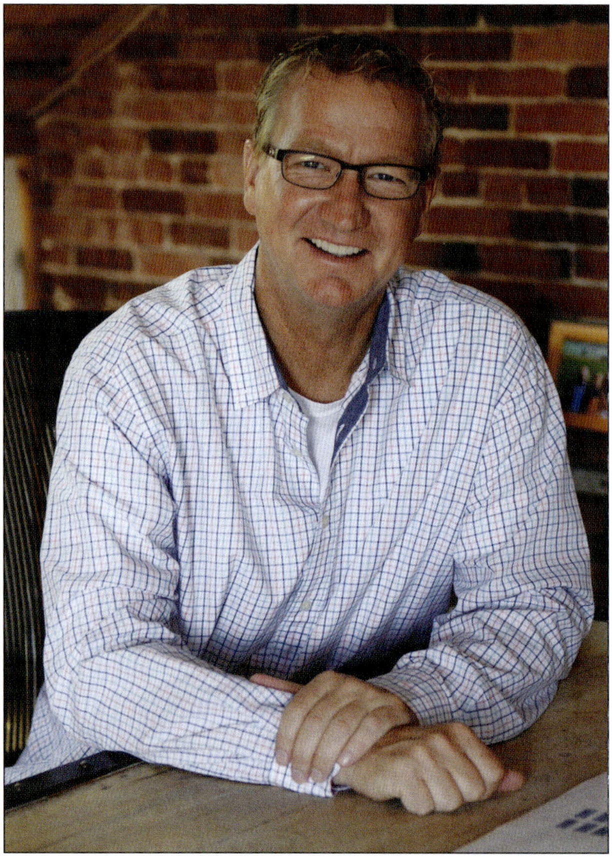

Dan Healey Jr. (pictured at left) started working for his father's company, AAP Inc., at 37 Water Street. Dan went to visit his father, Dan Sr., with his business plan at 26 years old, and ARC Technologies was born in 1988 on Cedar Street. The company grew rapidly. In 1995, he bought another location on Chestnut Street. ARC Technologies makes absorbing materials for defense and commercial customers. They manufacture cellphone applications to block electromagnetic interference signals with the technology. They employee roughly 140 people, and the facility on 37 Hunt Road, which is shown below, is 250,000 square feet. ARC Technologies is a family-oriented company; Dan knows all of his employees and their families. It is a big company with a family feel, and everything that Dan does is in memory of his father. (Both, photograph by Joey Walker; courtesy of Dan Healey.)

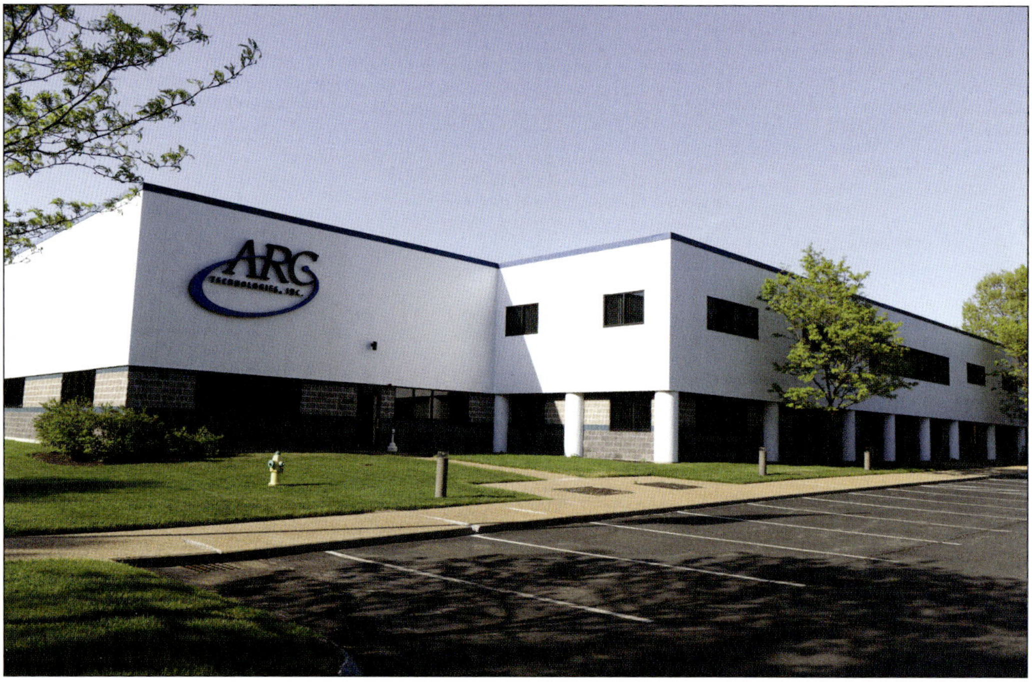

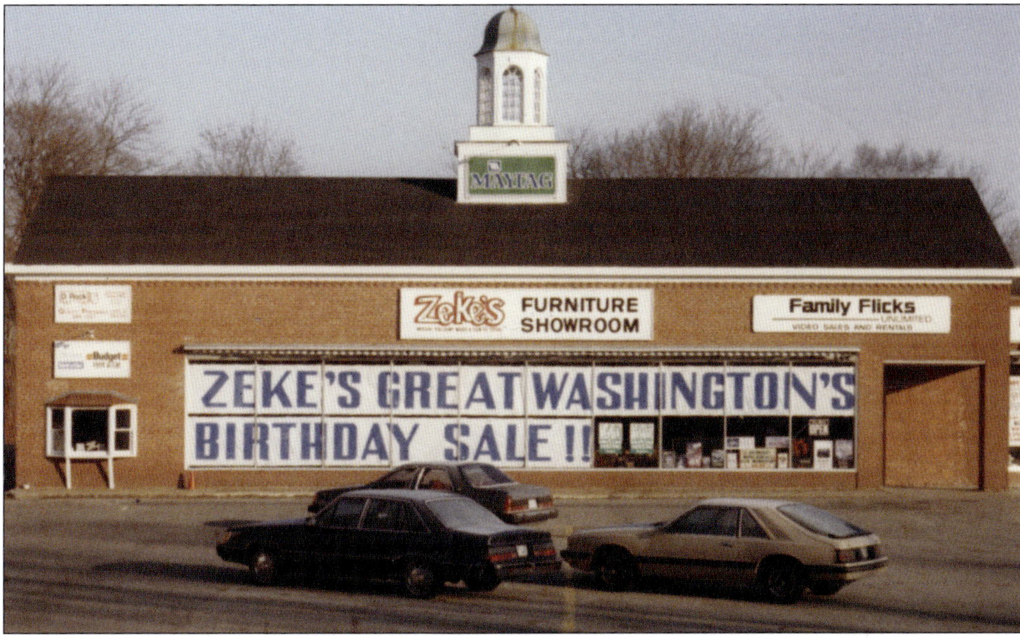

Zeke's Furniture Showroom ("Where you don't need a gun to steal") actually started as a yard sale at Steve Deorocki's home every weekend, and it soon became apparent that a more permanent place of business was needed. In 1975, space was rented on Oakland Street, and Zeke's was now official. It then moved to Haverhill Road to the A&P space. More furniture and appliances were added, with lines such as Eastern of Athol, Ther-a-pedic mattresses, and Maytag. In 1978, with the support of local banks and Mr. Solar himself, owner of the A&P, Deorocki bought the building. He was 23 years old. Deorocki and his father, Chet Deorocki, started D. Rock Air Freight and a used-car lot. In 1997, after negotiations, the building was sold to OSCO drug. Steve moved D. Rock Air Freight to Salisbury and was in business until 2012. (Both, courtesy of Steve Deorocki.)

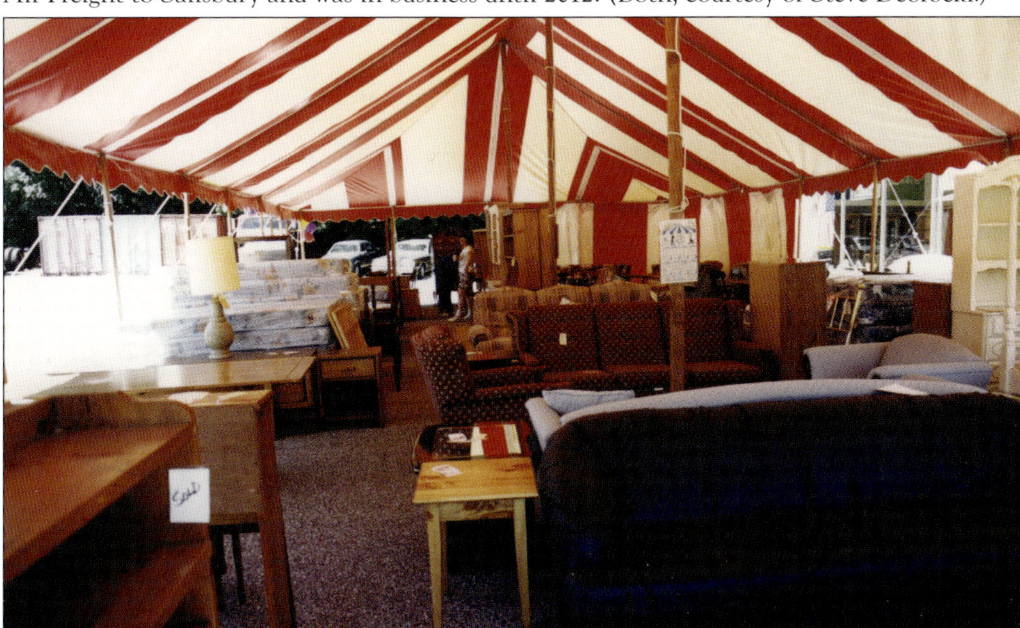

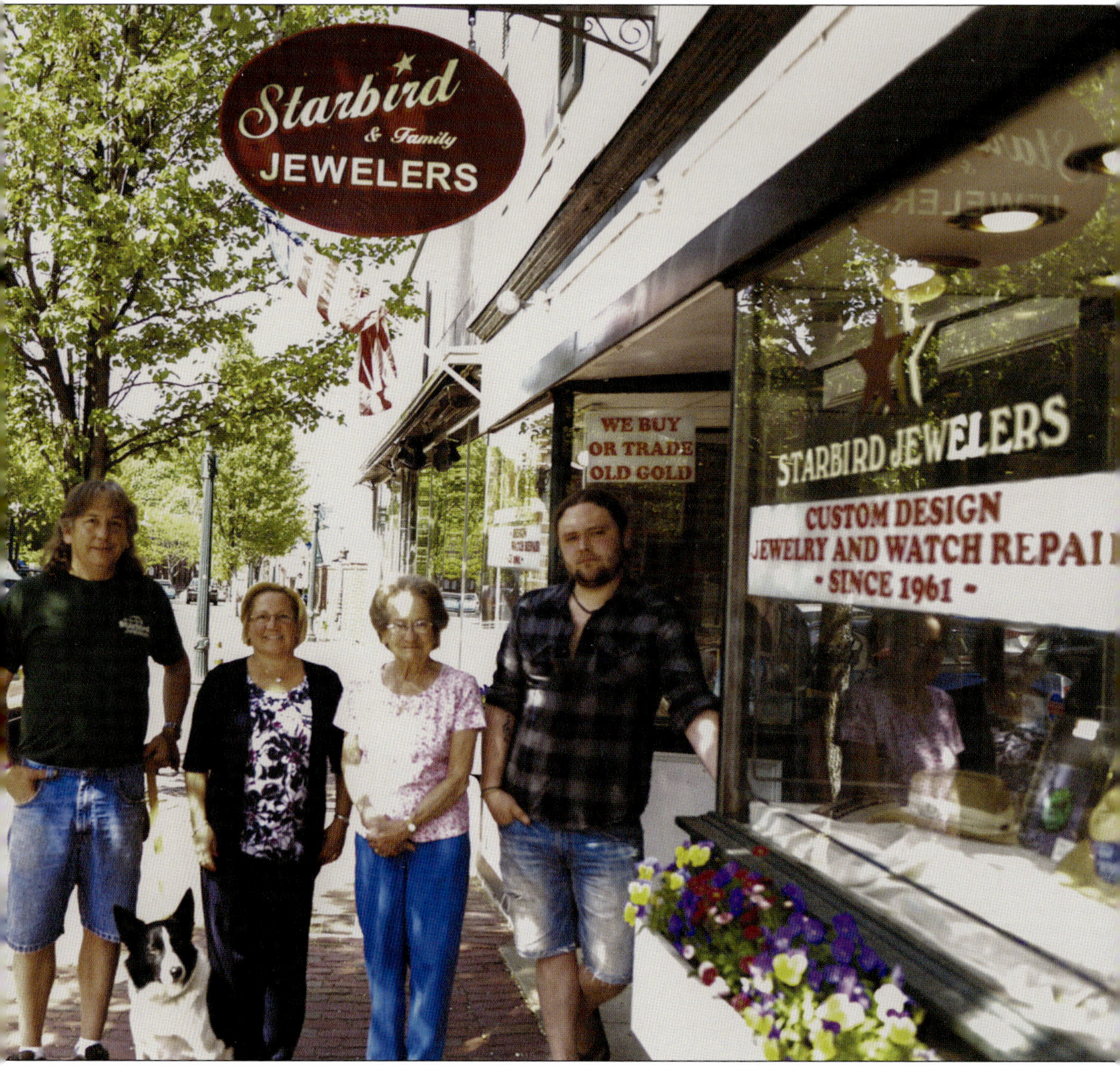

John Starbird and his wife, Netta, opened Starbird Jewelers in 1961. Starbird worked day and night to establish his business, repairing and customizing customers' orders. When it first opened, the shop was small, but as time went on, the Starbirds obtained the vacant shop next door. Their son Peter started working in the store when he was in high school. He watched his father over the years, learning how to fix watches and customize jewelry to satisfy the customer. In 2015, Netta, Peter, and his sister Dawn continue to run the shop with the same vision that John had when it first opened. Josh Welch also helps out in the store. Nico (the dog) is always there to greet customers. The way watches and jewelry are made may have changed over the years, but the one thing that has stayed the same is the way the Starbirds treat their customers as family and appreciate their loyalty. (Photograph by Joey Walker.)

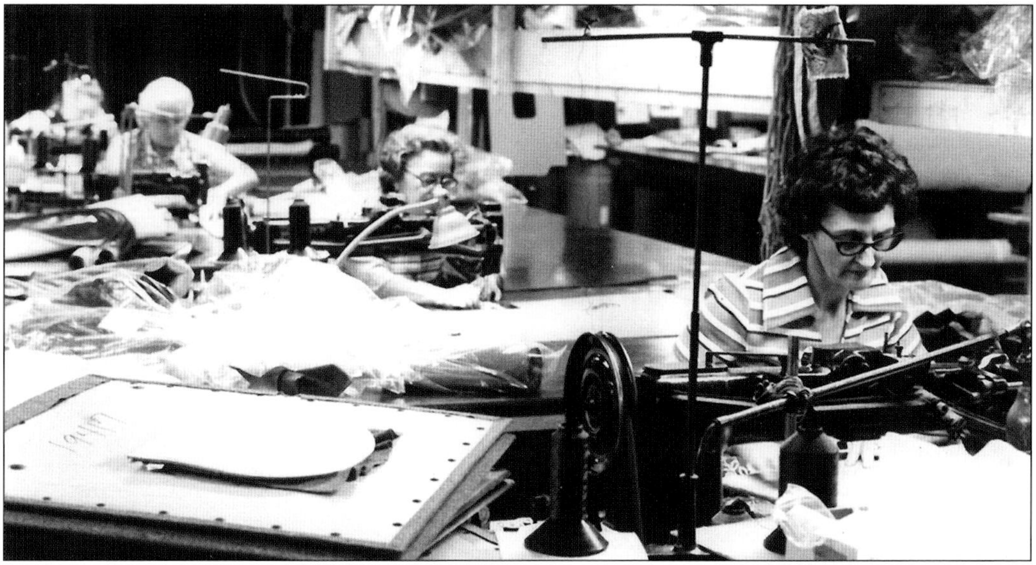

LeBaron Bonney has over 50 years' experience producing award-winning automobile interiors for antique and custom restoration. The company designs and manufactures kits that a trim shop or individual can use to install a new interior. In 1938, Lee Atherton and his brother Jack opened a bicycle-rental business on Cape Cod. They named the business LeBaron Bonney Company. It evolved from renting bicycles into a mail business offering historical and decorative maps and model sailing vessels. After World War II, LeBaron Bonney produced new upholstered furniture and provided reupholstering services for the future family business. In 1959, Lee Atherton purchased a 1930 Model A Deluxe Roadster to restore. When he looked for someone to upholster the seats, he could not find a place. One of his workers suggested that they duplicate the original interior of the car and top. In 1965, the company purchased a 14,000-square-foot facility in Amesbury. It needed more space and added the old Biddle and Smart building to its facility, providing another 29,000 square feet. (Both, courtesy of Scott Holbrook and LeBaron Bonney.)

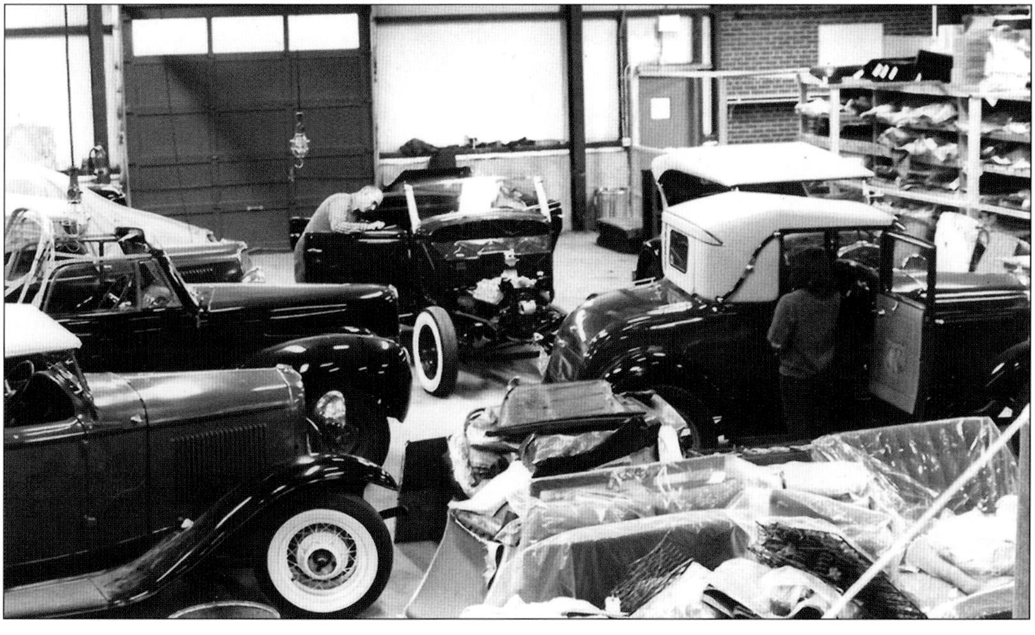

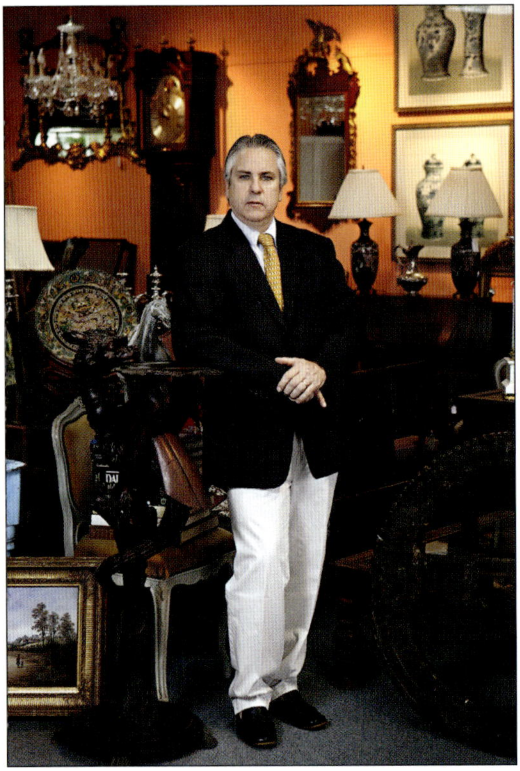

John McInnis Auctioneer was founded in 1978. McInnis is one of the leading auctioneers in New England, selling art and antiques throughout the United States and the rest of the world. His auction of Pres. John Kennedy's collection brought many people to Amesbury to see the fabulous memorabilia. McInnis loves helping people find antique treasures. His sister and brothers all are involved in their own antique businesses, and their father shared his knowledge and love of antiques with them. (Courtesy of John McInnis.)

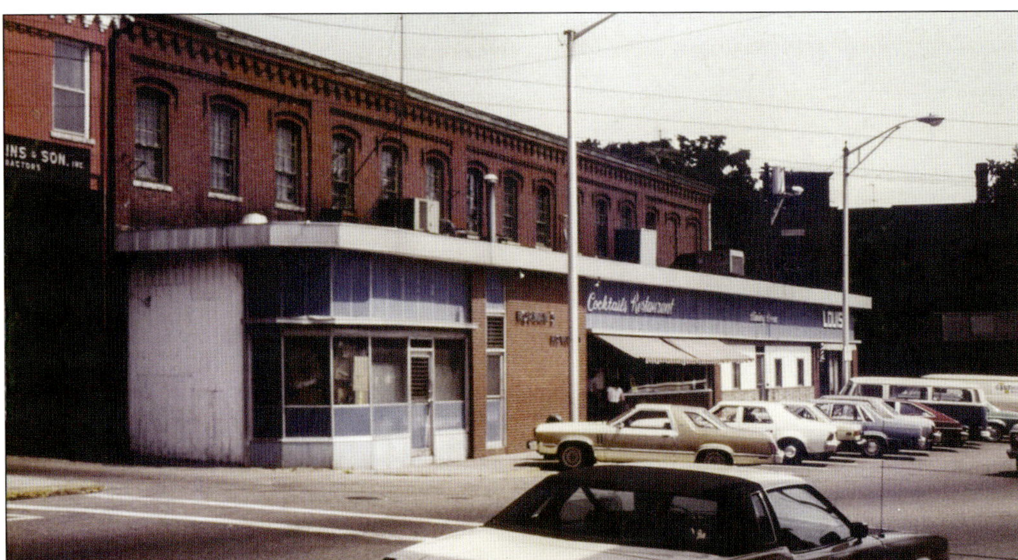

Norman's Restaurant was the cornerstone of downtown Amesbury. Norman Pelletier started working for his stepfather Marty Melia at White Lunch in 1950. When Melia passed away, Pelletier took over the restaurant. In 1963, he changed the name to Norman's. On December 5, 1984, the doors were closed with much fanfare. With the autographed menus and souvenir beer mugs, people took away some of Amesbury's history. Dr. Messner and his family were the honored recipients of the last meal served at Norman's. (Courtesy of the Amesbury Public Library.)

Patricia "Pat" and Jim Perry opened Carriagetown Chocolates in April 2005. They have all kinds of everyday and holiday confectionaries, coffee, and gift items. Easter is a busy time, with Pat creating her famous Easter baskets. She is involved with Lucy's Love Bus and sponsors Savannah, a little girl with cancer. Since 2010, Pat and her customers have donated $4,500 directly for Savannah's care. (Photograph by Joey Walker.)

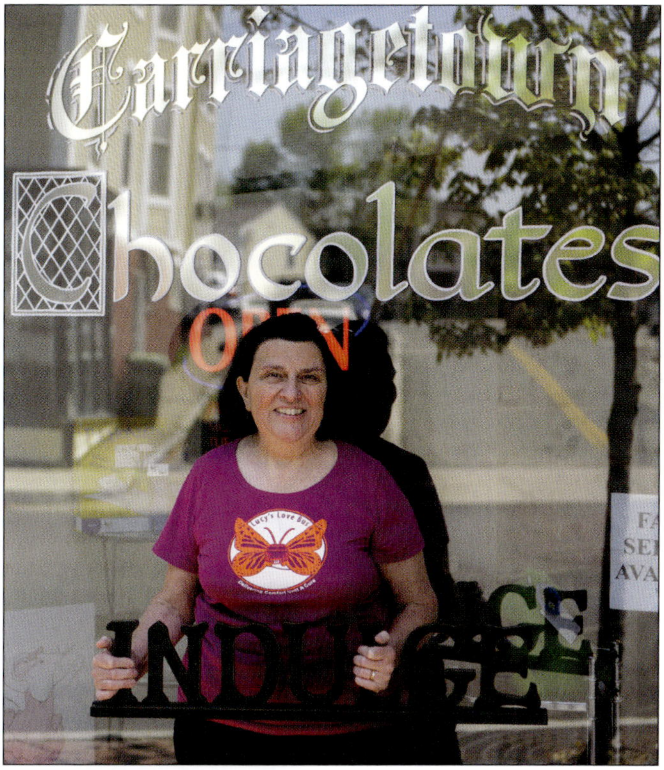

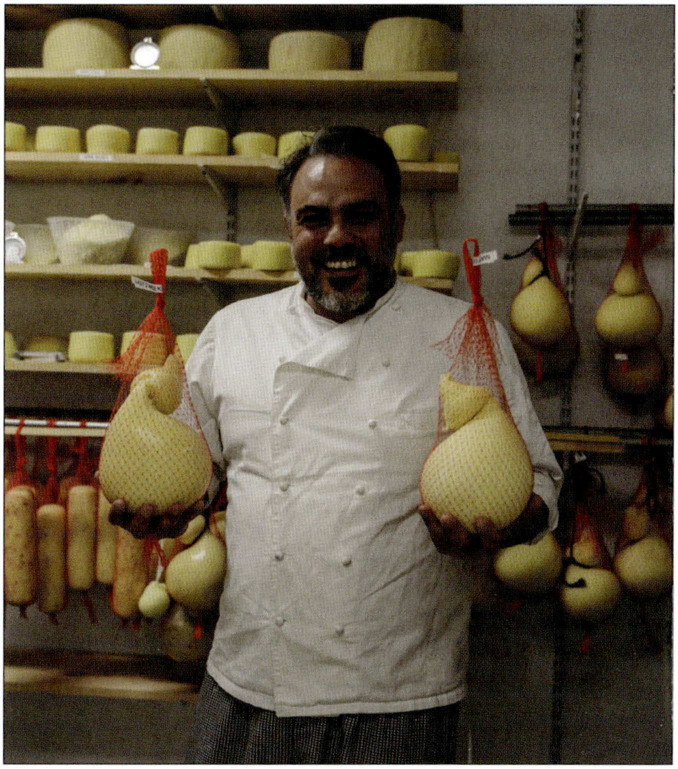

Wolf Meadow Farm, owned by Luca Mignogna, opened on October 27, 2013. Mignogna was born in Campobasso, Italy, and he learned many lessons from his family, specifically that life comes from the earth. He is passionate about sustainable production and will only use high-quality milk from local dairies that practice sustainable farming and humane treatment of the dairy cattle. He brings his cheeses to farmers' markets and loves to share his passion for cheese-making, offering classes to the public. (Photograph by Joey Walker.)

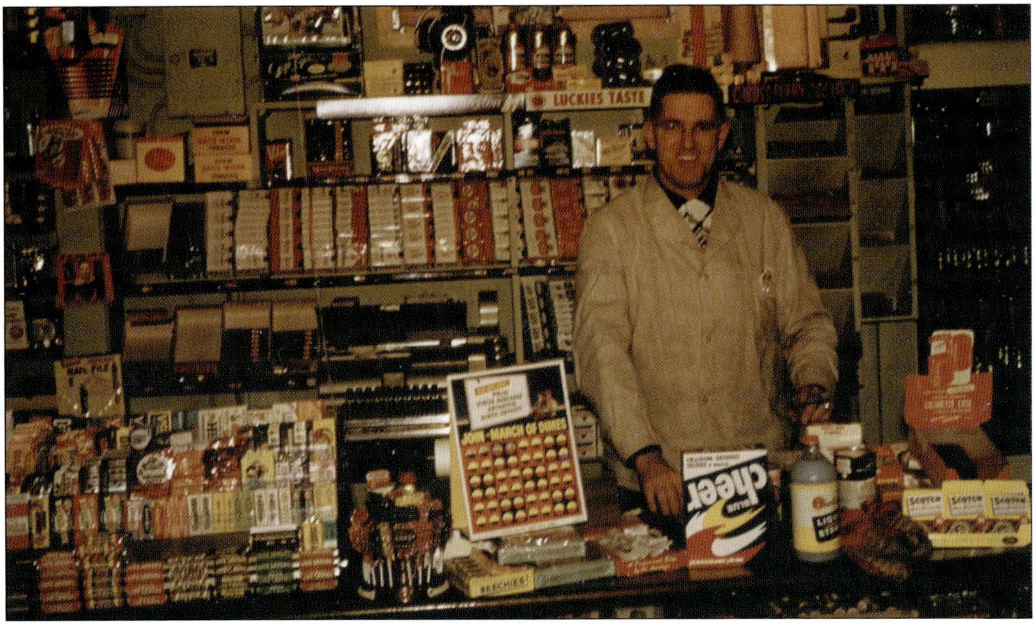

Ted's Neighborhood Store opened in 1954. Ted and Muriel White ran the business in addition to raising four children, Glenda, Peg, Tom, and Carol, all of whom worked in the store at one time or another. Ted was also a substitute mailman, school bus driver, and volunteer fireman. Carol said, "I can see that the four of us were the big winners. The whole experience of being part of a family business made us who we are today." Customers remember telling Ted and Muriel to put their purchases on account and going around the counter to select their own penny candy. It was a true neighborhood store. If someone called Ted at 10:00 p.m. and said they needed something, he would go back to the store so that they could get it. The store closed in 1976. (Both, courtesy of Carol Metcalf.)

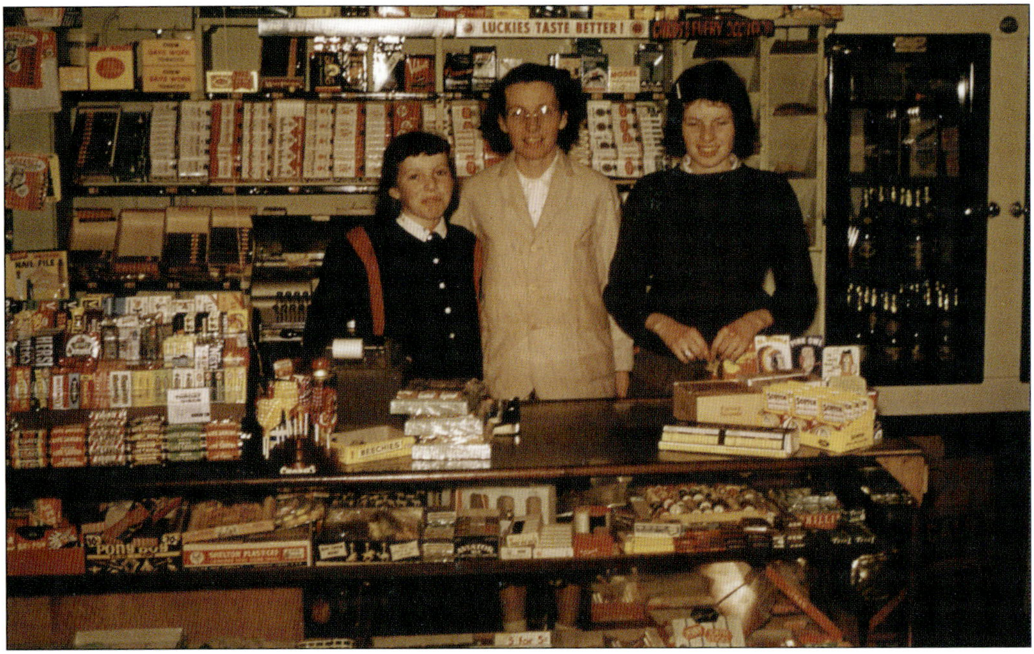

Two

Making a Difference

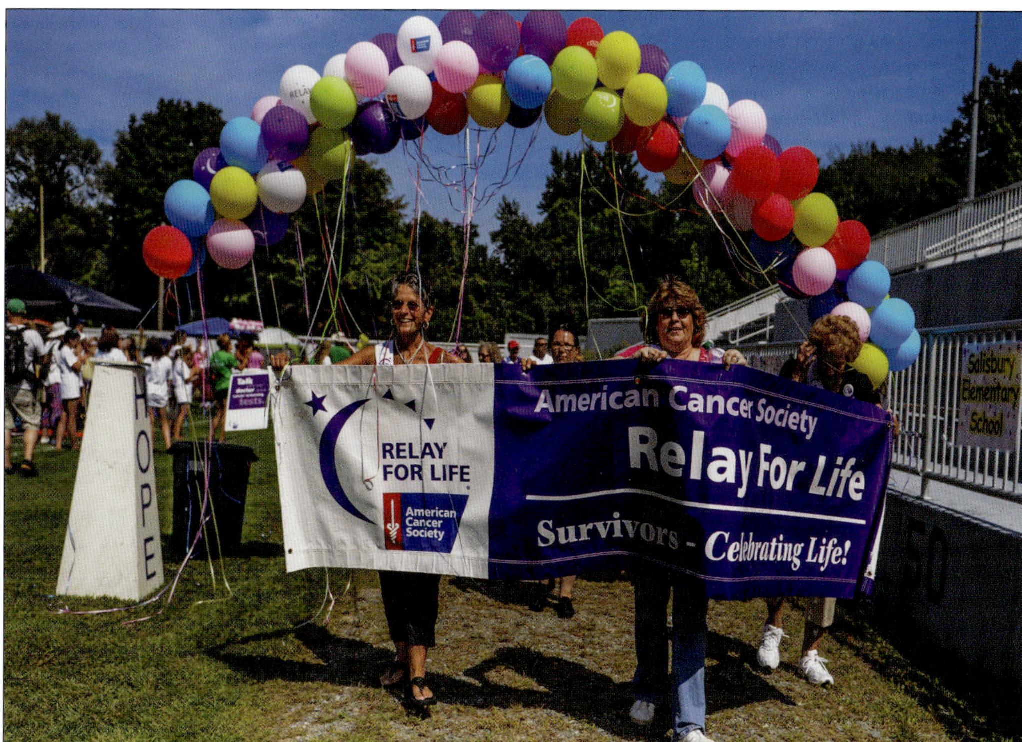

Amesbury Relay for Life was established in 2002. Relay for Life is an opportunity to raise money and awareness about cancer. The first lap of the race is for survivors and caregivers, seen above in 2013, and the 14-hour event brings Landry Stadium alive with music, food, theme laps, and entertainment. The luminaria ceremony is about people that lost their battle, are fighting the battle, and survived the battle; the lights are turned off, candles are lit, and all of those cancer has affected are remembered. (Photograph by Joey Walker.)

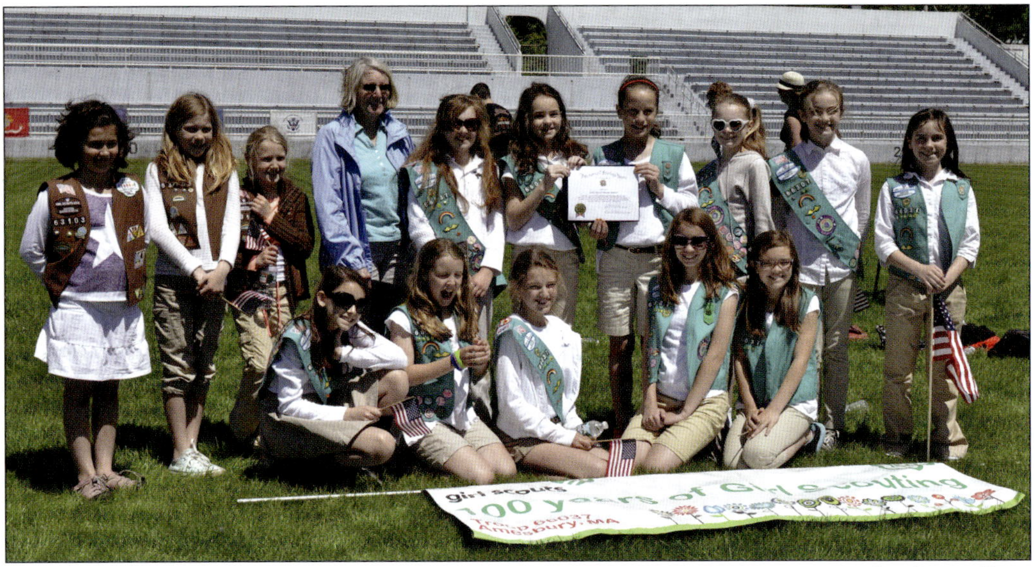

These Girl Scouts have twice been recognized by the Veterans of Foreign Wars for their efforts collecting cookie donations as well as other needed items (toiletries, lip balm, and candy) and sending them, along with handmade cards, to the troops in 2013. Pictured here are (first row) Rachel Bucher, Meghan McElaney, Katelyn Brannelly, Izze Wetherbee, and Lily O'Neill; (second row) Katelyn Flaherty, Anna Bailey, Rosie Costello, Karen Iworsky, Celia Celona, Hannah Doran, Ceara Cronin, Rylee Dalton, Alanna O'Reilly, and Sarah McCarthy. (Photograph by Joey Walker.)

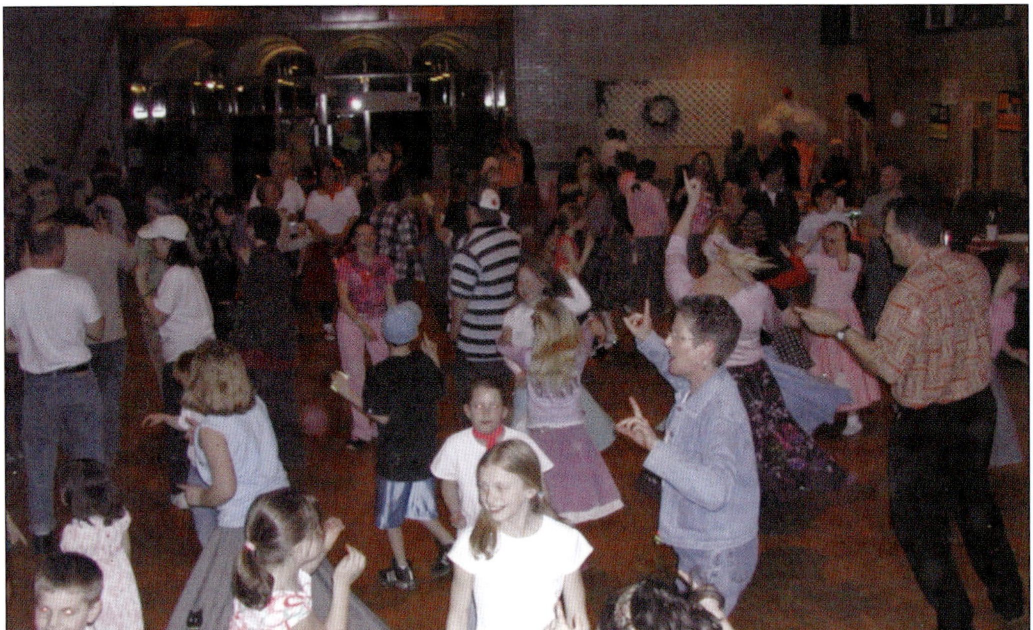

In 2005, the Amesbury Public Library held a 1950s-themed dance fundraiser for the Jefferson Parish Library, which was devastated during Hurricane Katrina. They had volunteers making root beer floats, pizza donated by local businesses, and a disc jockey that played 1950s music. They raised $3,600 for the Jefferson Parish Library. (Photograph by the author.)

Colin McBride was 16 years old when he presented his Eagle Scout project to the Amesbury Improvement Association. McBride wanted to restore the damaged powder house that was built in 1810, used to store powder and shot during the War of 1812. He needed to estimate how long the project would take and what materials would be needed, contact a mason to ask how to fix the holes that were in the structure, get volunteers to help him complete the project, and create a budget. Due to the remoteness of the location, they needed to use a gas-powered generator and a fire hydrant for water. McBride's project helped preserve a historical landmark with the assistance of the Amesbury Improvement Association, which works tirelessly to make the city a better place. (Both, courtesy of Colin, Doug, and Rose McBride.)

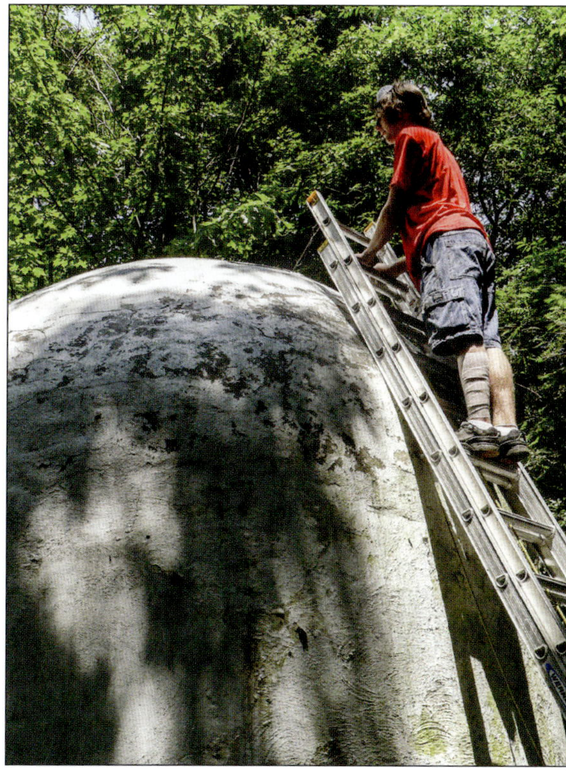

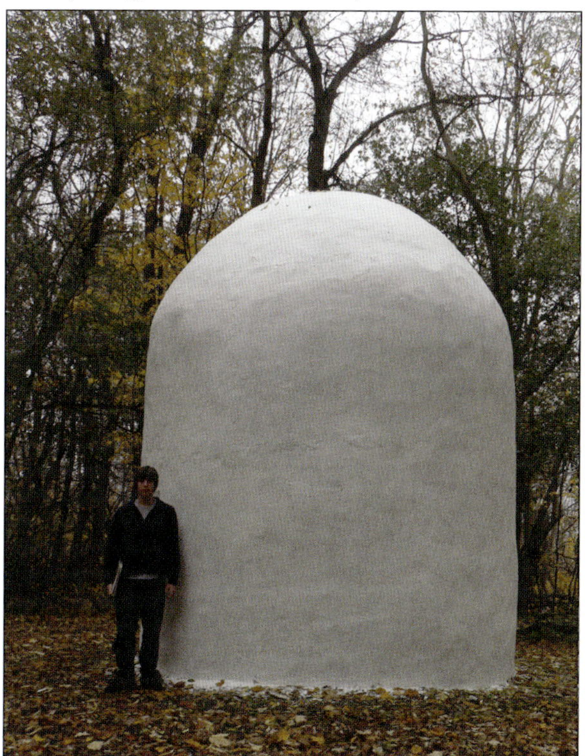

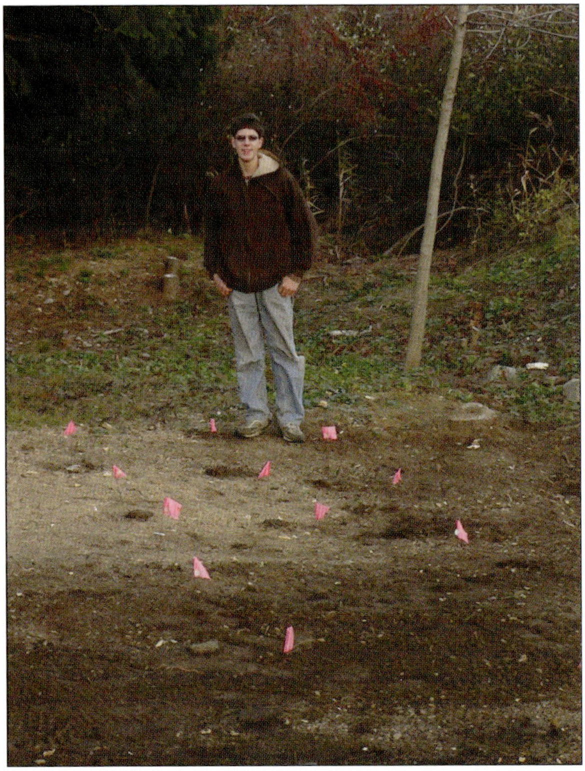

Matthew McBride, a member of the Holy Family Parish, wanted his Eagle Scout project to benefit his parish community. His project was to restore the section of St. Joseph's Cemetery that was devoted to unbaptized babies during the 1960s. During this time period, babies that died unbaptized were not allowed to be buried in the main cemetery and relegated to the border of the burial ground. There are very few records of the burials, so the number of graves is unknown. The area was overgrown, and he cut down trees and cleared the leaves, brush, and trash that had collected over the last 40 years. McBride believed that restoring the cemetery would provide comfort to the families whose children were buried there, knowing their children are respected and acknowledged. He believes that the most important aspect of this project is bringing recognition to the human souls that are buried in this area. (Both, courtesy of Matthew McBride.)

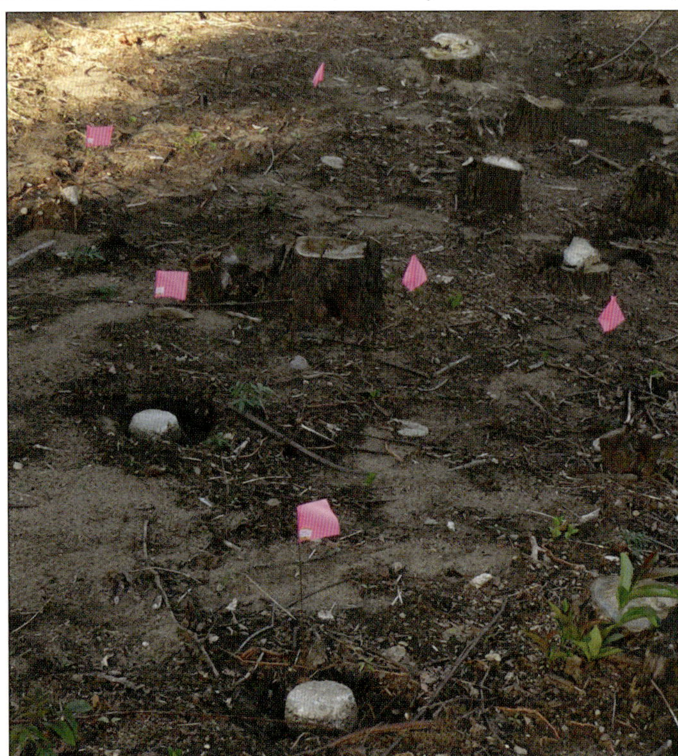

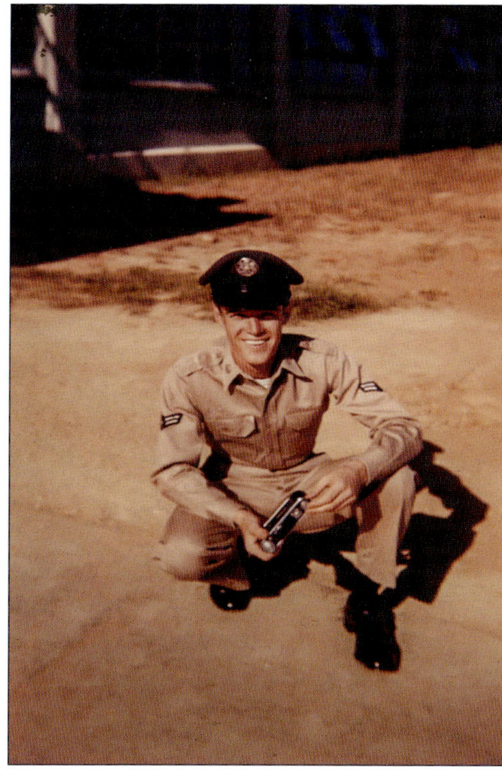

Robert Kelleher entered the Air Force on March 6, 1957, and he went to Lackland Air Force Base in San Antonio, Texas, for basic training. He left basic training on June 1, 1957, as an airman third class and went on to Keesler Air Force Base in Biloxi, Mississippi. Kelleher studied radio intercept, and he graduated from radio school in December 1957. After a 30-day leave, he went to Crete, Greece, and stayed there until January 1959. Kelleher then went to Fort Meade in Maryland and was assigned to the National Security Agency, but he never got the chance to work there, as he was sent to Sembach Air Force Base in Germany. He separated from the Air Force on February 15, 1961, at Maguire Air Force Base in New Jersey. (Right, courtesy of Robert Kelleher; below, photograph by Joey Walker.)

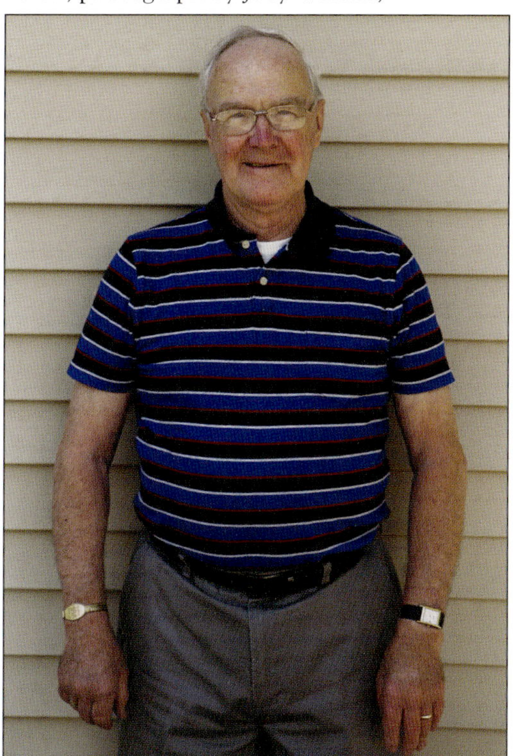

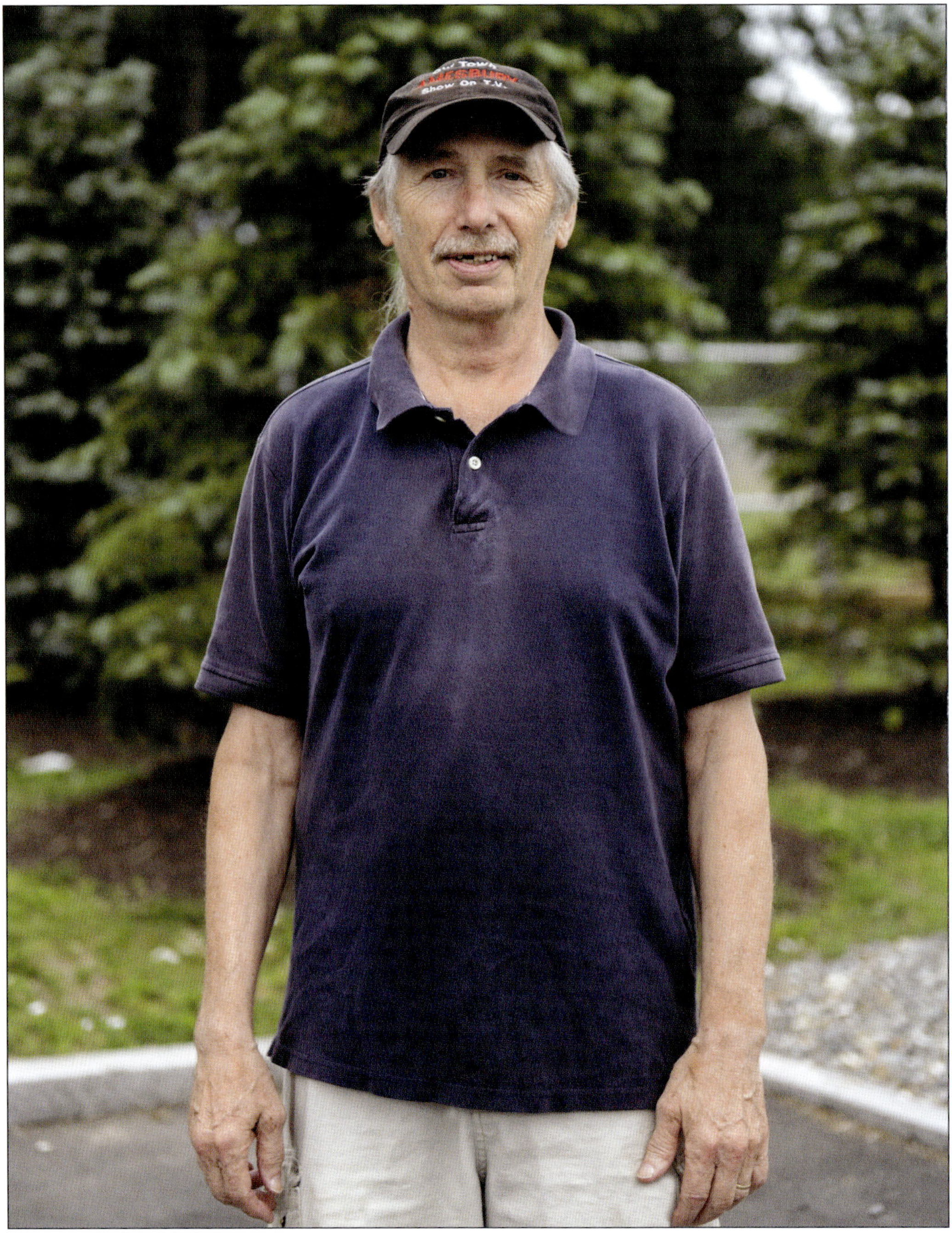

Our Town, a cable show created by Larry Frost, first went on air in 2007. Frost's goal for the show is to help future generations see what life was like in Amesbury: how people took care of each other, people smiling, sharing, and maybe seeing a relative or two. Frost would like to reach everyone, but his concentration is on the elderly, sick, and people too busy. Having the show available online allows people to "come home" whenever they want. In addition to hosting *Our Town*, Frost is also a licensed massage therapist. His personal passions are healing and slowing people down to enjoy the beauty of life around them. (Photograph by Joey Walker.)

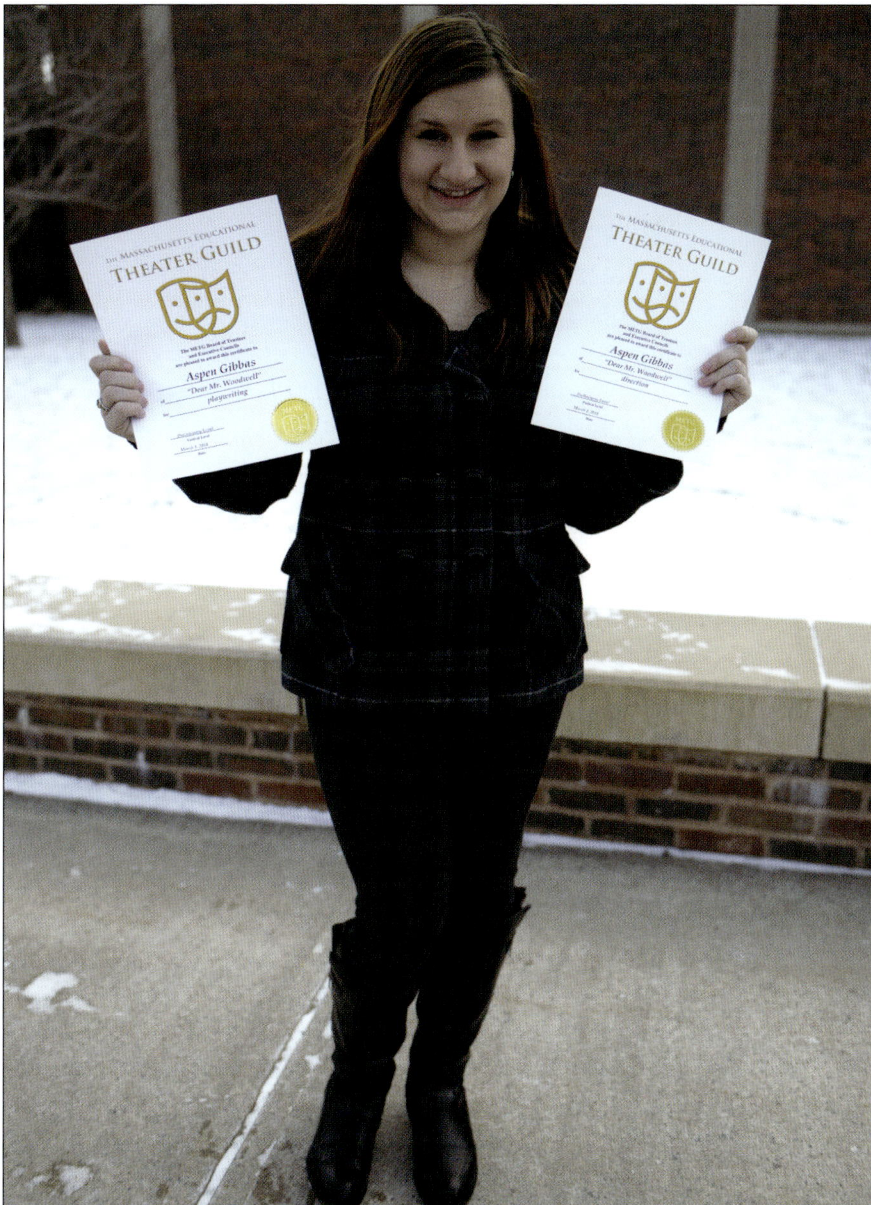

Aspen Gibbas was introduced to the Woodwell letters in her junior year of high school, as her class used the letters in their study of World War II. The letters were written to Roland Woodwell from former students that were overseas during World War II. Gibbas decided to write a play and bring the soldiers to life. After a year of writing, typing up letters, researching, and finding relatives, she presented her first draft of the script *Dear Mr. Woodwell* to the Amesbury High School Drama Club. Their first performance was held on February 27, 2014. The cast and crew took their show to the preliminaries of the Massachusetts Educational Theatre Guild Drama Festival. They won awards for costume and sound design, and Gibbas won awards for directing and playwriting. The group advanced to the semifinal round of Dramafest, but sadly, they did not win. Aspen Gibbas is currently studying theater at the Playwrights Horizons Theater School at Tisch School of the Arts in New York. (Photograph by Joey Walker.)

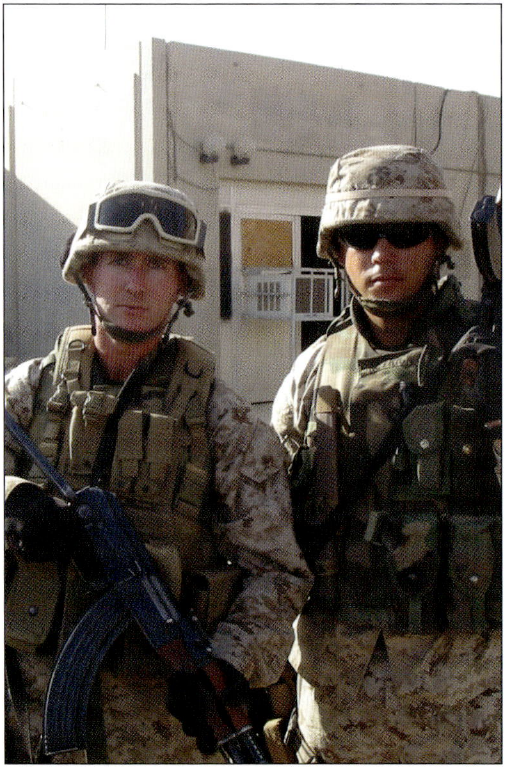

Greg Iworsky (pictured left and below, standing third from left) enlisted in the Marine Corps after high school, and in 2004 and 2005, he served as an infantry squad leader in Iraq. His unit, known as the "Bounty Hunter Squad," conducted patrols, cordons, and searches. They went on over 100 patrols and detained more than 100 men, most of whom were insurgents, smugglers, or illegal persons. For his actions in Iraq, Iworsky was awarded the Navy/Marine Corps Achievement Medal for valor in combat: "For heroic achievement while serving as an infantry squad leader . . . During a deliberate attack on the platoon's position, Sergeant Iworsky took the initiative to maneuver his squad to reinforce the platoon's defensive positions and, without hesitation or instruction, directed accurate and deadly machine gun fire on the enemy position . . . His actions were instrumental to the unit's successful identification and detainment of a Division High Value Target." During his tour, Iworsky's squad saw intense action, and of the 12 men in his unit, two were killed and six wounded. (Both, courtesy of Dennis "Ski" Iworsky.)

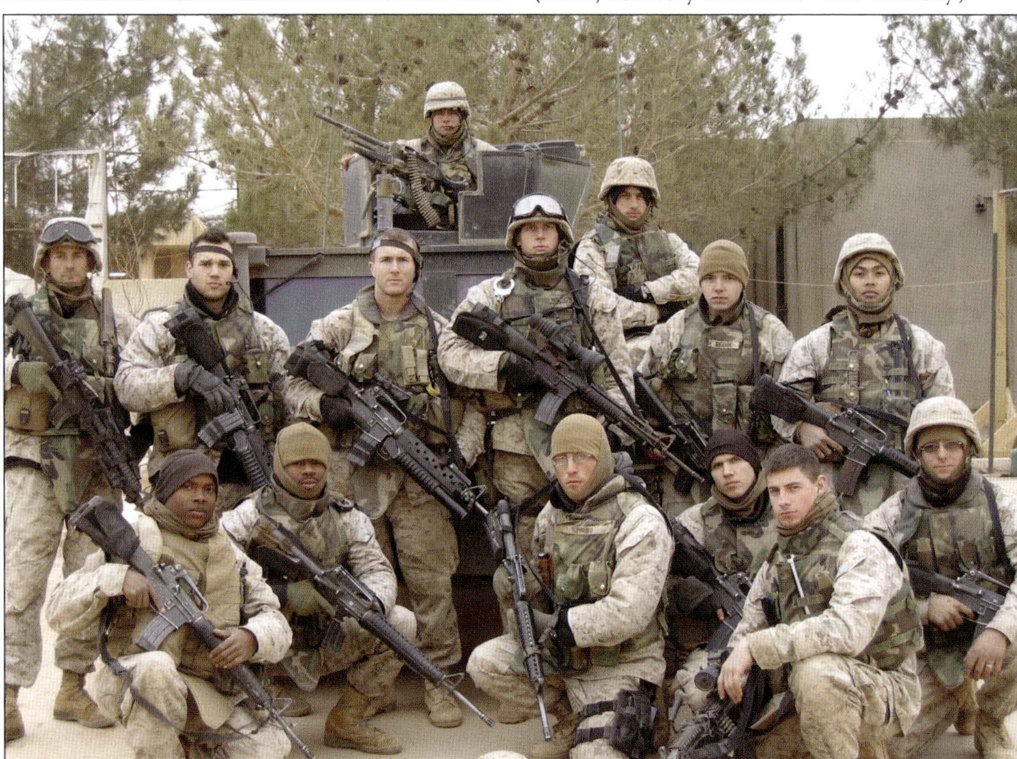

Marine sergeant Dennis "Ski" Iworsky spent 20 months in Vietnam in 1968 and 1969. He served many years as the post quartermaster for VFW Post 2016. He is a member of the American Legion, Disabled American Veterans, and Ukrainian-American Veterans. He helped organize local patriotic events, including the Support the Troops Christmas dinner for troops who were home for Christmas, the Amesbury Memorial Day Ceremony, and the Cashman School's From America with Love program, which was organized by his wife, Karen. That program shipped over 1,000 parcels to the troops serving in Iraq and Afghanistan. He is a cochairman of the citizen group Amesbury Veterans' Memorials Restoration Committee, which helped to restore the Amesbury doughboy in 2014 and the Amesbury Civil War Memorial in 2015. He has also been appointed to the Amesbury Trustees of War Memorials. (Both, courtesy of Dennis "Ski" Iworsky.)

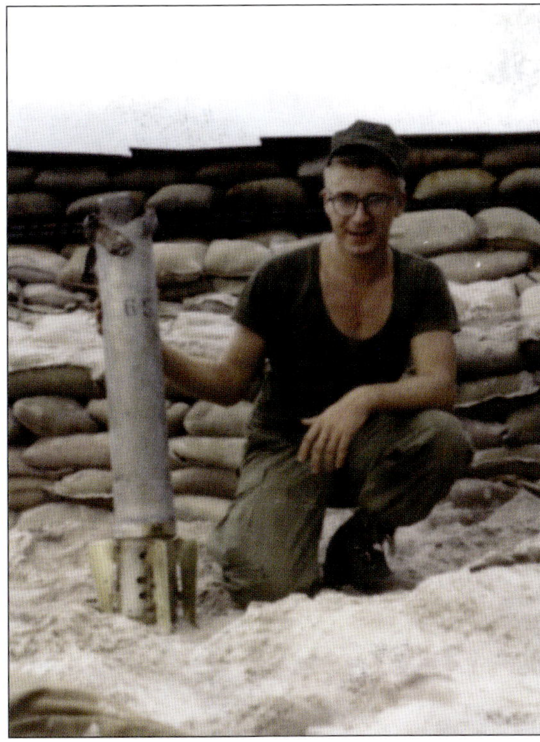

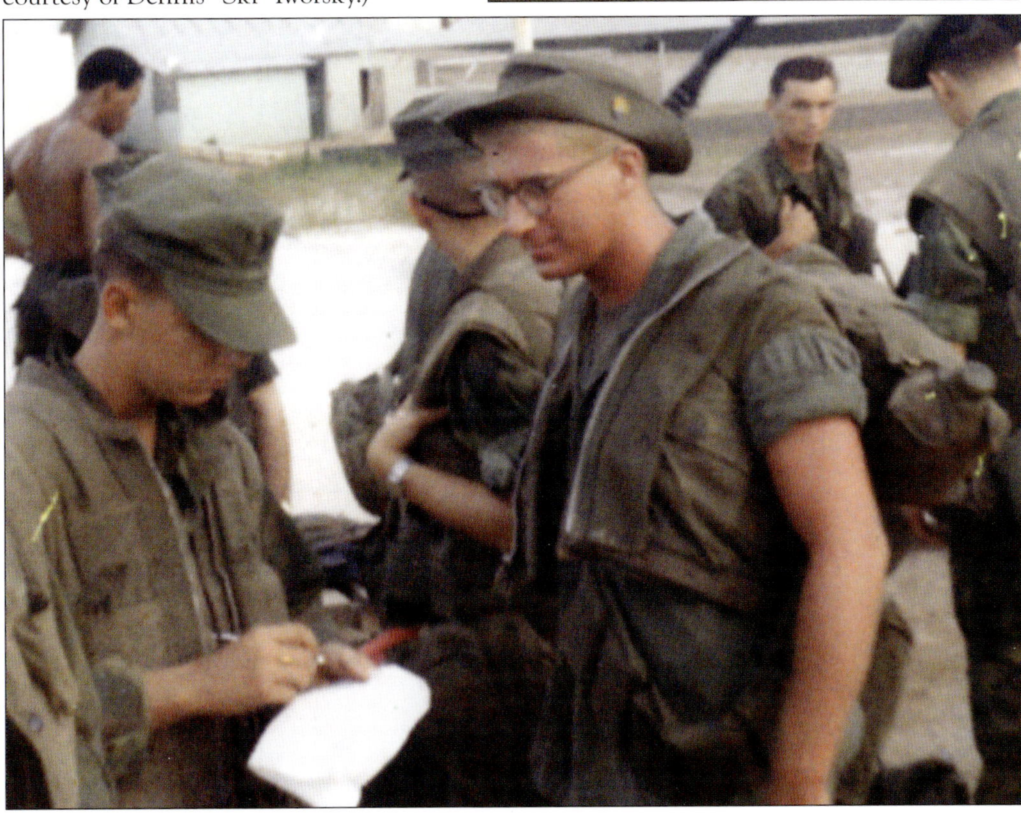

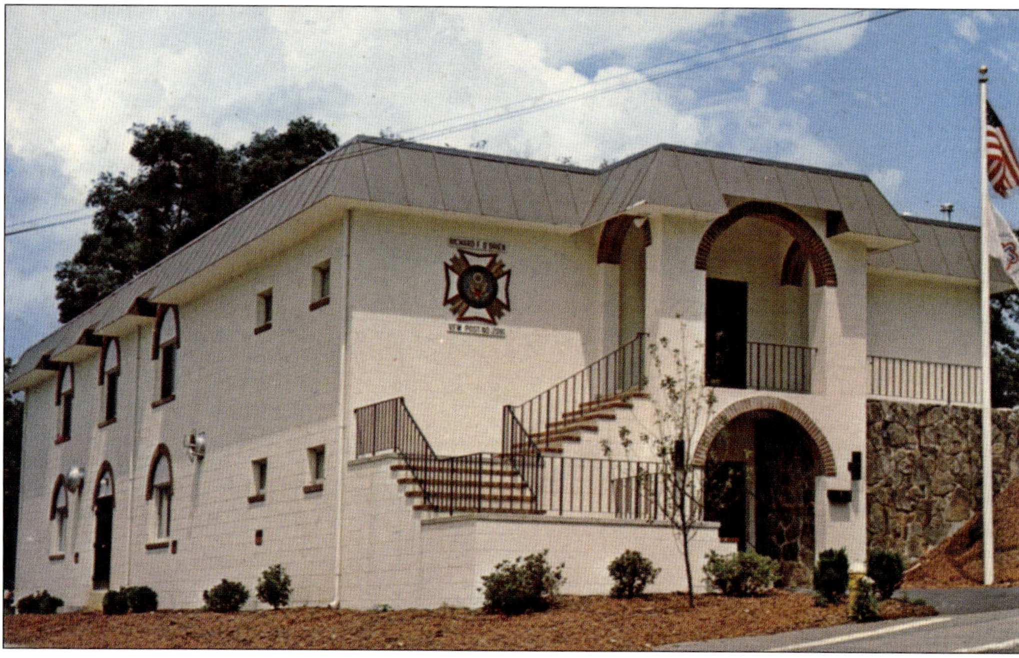

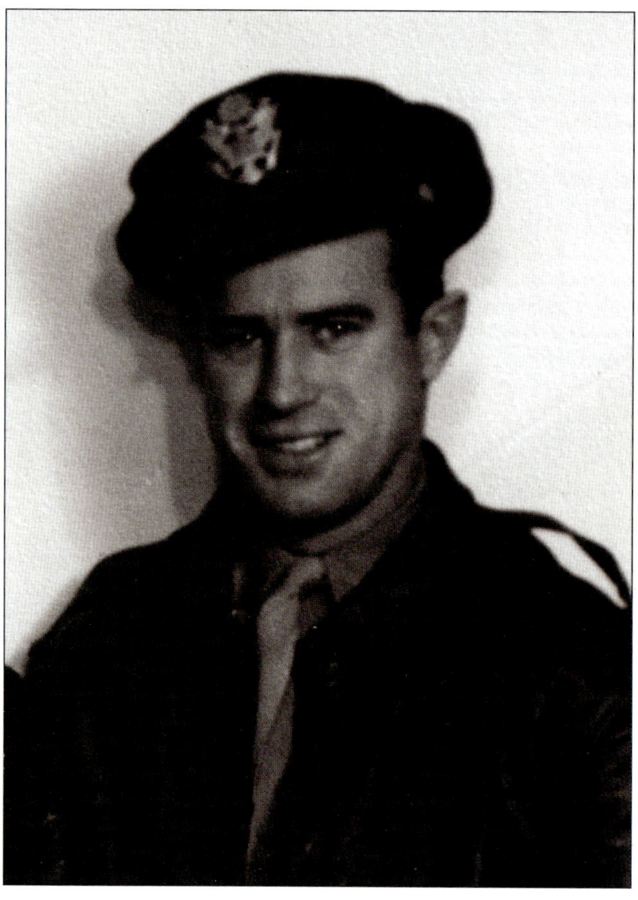

Richard Francis O'Brien was born in Amesbury in 1920. He joined the US Army Air Force as a flight officer, was assigned to the B-29 Bomber *City of Cleveland* as the radar operator, and then stationed in Guam. On June 7, 1945, the radar operator of the *City of College Park* was ill, so O'Brien filled in for him. After completing their bombing run over Japan, they headed back to Guam. Approximately 100 miles out, the plane ran out of fuel and was ditched into the Pacific Ocean. Of the crew of 11, only eight survived, and O'Brien's body was never recovered. He was awarded several medals, including the Air Medal and the Purple Heart. O'Brien is memorialized on the *Courts of the Missing* in Honolulu's Punchbowl Cemetery. VFW Post 2016 was renamed the Richard F. O'Brien Post in February 1946. The new VFW building was dedicated in 1978. (Above, courtesy of the Amesbury Public Library; left, courtesy of Sheila Zindroski.)

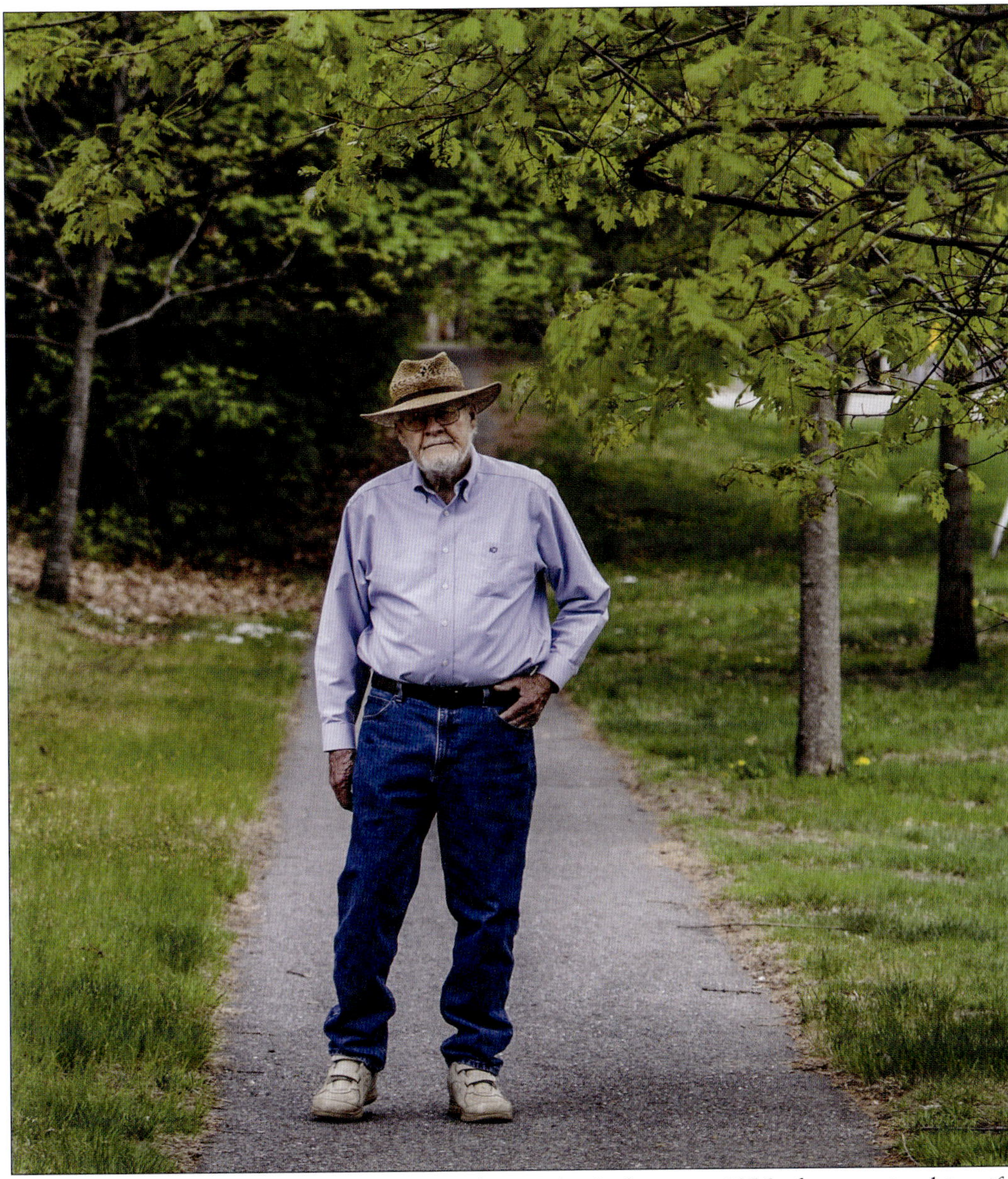

Richard Gale moved to Amesbury from Indianapolis, Indiana, in 1996 after meeting his wife, Annie Tunstall. Impressed by the history of Amesbury, Gale founded Amesbury Treasures and has received the Pioneer Partnership award from Essex National Heritage and the Outstanding Citizen Forester Award. He is on the boards of the Amesbury Carriage Museum and Amesbury Treasures and served as the president of the Bartlett Museum. A landscape architect, Gale served on the tree board for eight years and organized the planting of over 1,000 trees, and he worked with crews to cleanup the Back River and Alliance Park. An active attendee of the Friends Meeting House, he served as the building committee's clerk. The Amesbury Council of Churches honored him with its Citizen of the Year award. He restarted the ice-skating rink and founded History Day at Amesbury Middle School. This modern-day Johnny Appleseed loves the trees on Route 110 running up the hill from Cumberland Farm, shown here in 2015. (Photograph by Joey Walker; courtesy of Annie Tunstall and Richard Gale.)

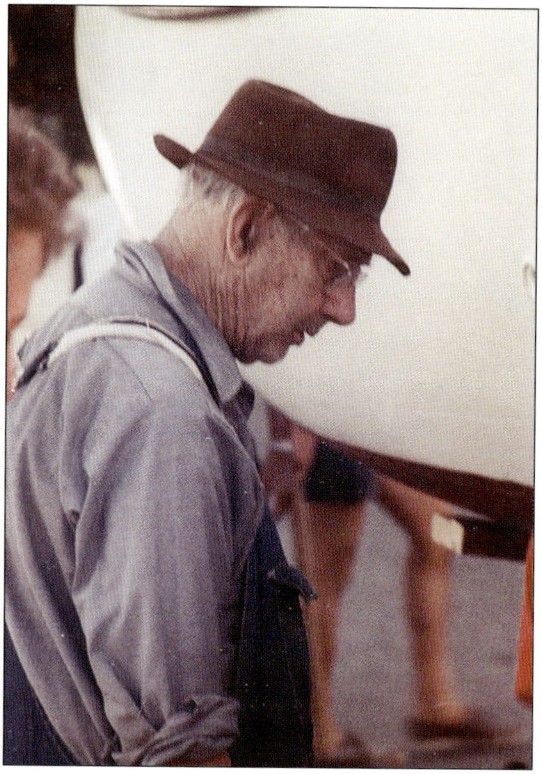

Myron Cowden was born in 1899, and he began working in the automobile industry as a woodworker in the early 1930s. In the late 1930s, Cowden started a boat shop on Merrimac Street, and there he began his legacy in boat building. During World War II, he worked for Sims Brothers, building 110-foot wooden submarine chasers for the Navy. After the war, he continued making many S.S. Crocker–designed sailboats, including two for himself, both named *For Winds*. He built a 40-foot Walter McGinnis cruiser for David C. Bailey. Cowden died in December 1993, and his ashes were spread in the 100-fathom-deep water off the Isle of Shoals by a few close friends. Anthony Noon bought and ran his shop for a few years until his passing. In Jeff Picard's years of woodworking he has met many people, including two presidents, but no one has impacted his life more than Myron Cowden. (Both, photograph by Paula Noon; courtesy of Jeff Picard.)

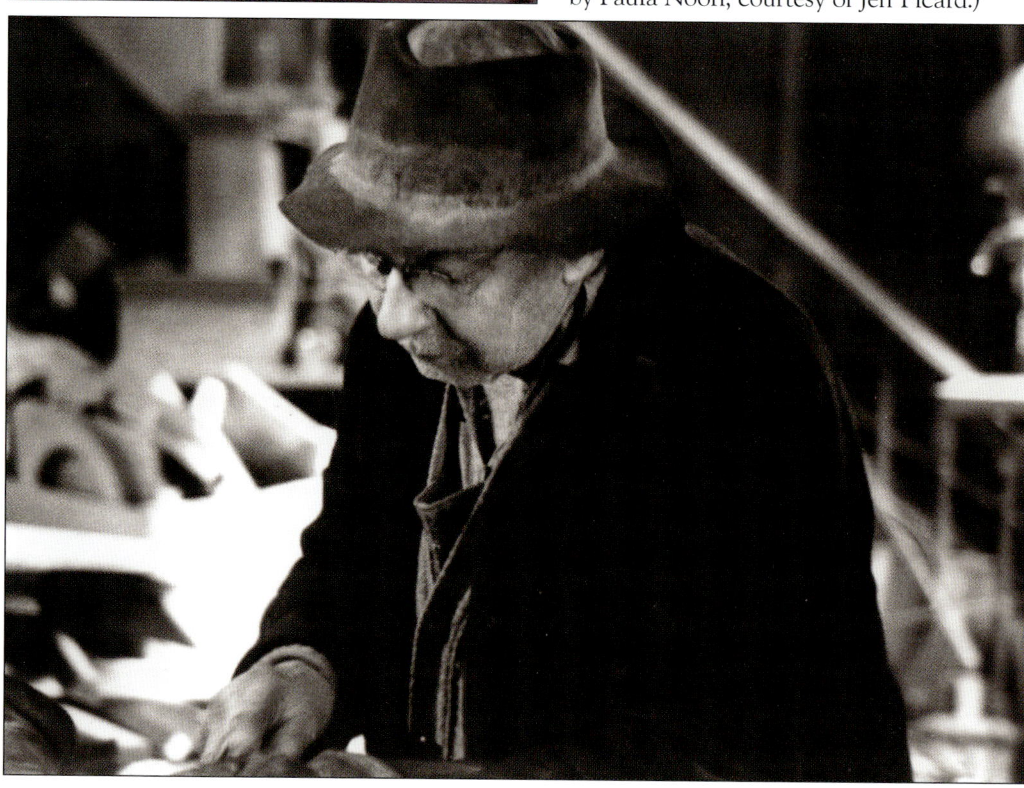

Three

Parks and Recreation

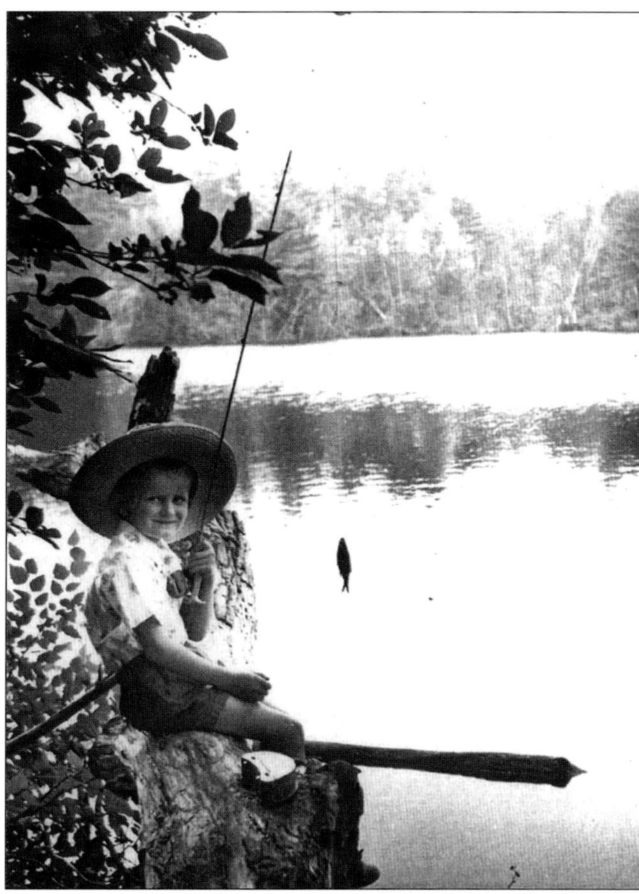

Amesbury has a lot of lakes, ponds, and rivers to select from to find the best place to fish: Lake Gardner, Lake Attitash, Tuxbury Pond, the Powow River, and the Merrimack River. This little boy is enjoying a summer day fishing in the lake. He is proudly showing his catch of the day. (Courtesy of the Amesbury Public Library.)

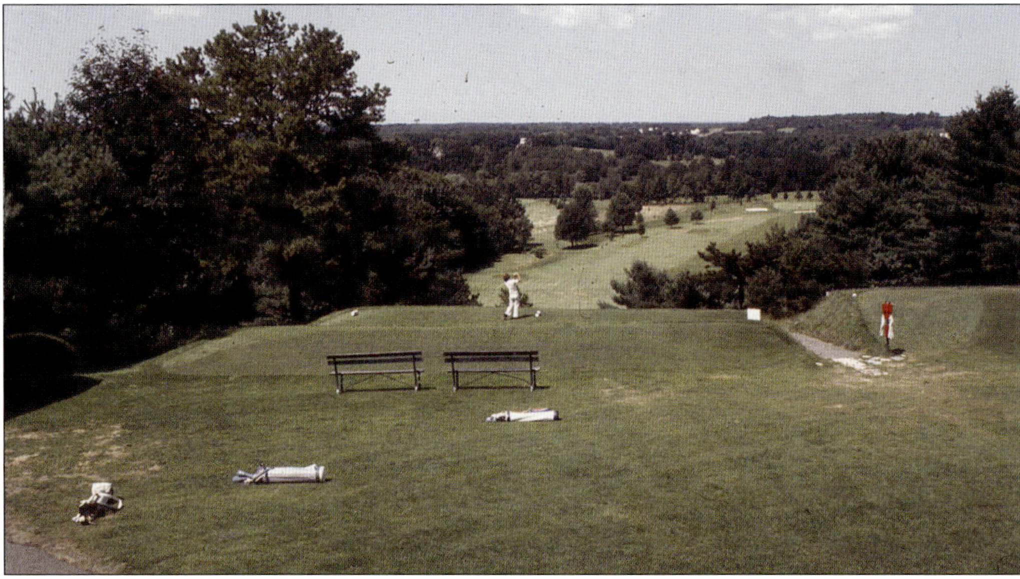

The Amesbury Country Club opened in 1922, and it was members only until 1960. When the Mellon family bought the club, they opened it to the public. John Greenleaf Whittier's poem "The Fountain" was written from the top of the hill of the course. (Courtesy of the Amesbury Public Library.)

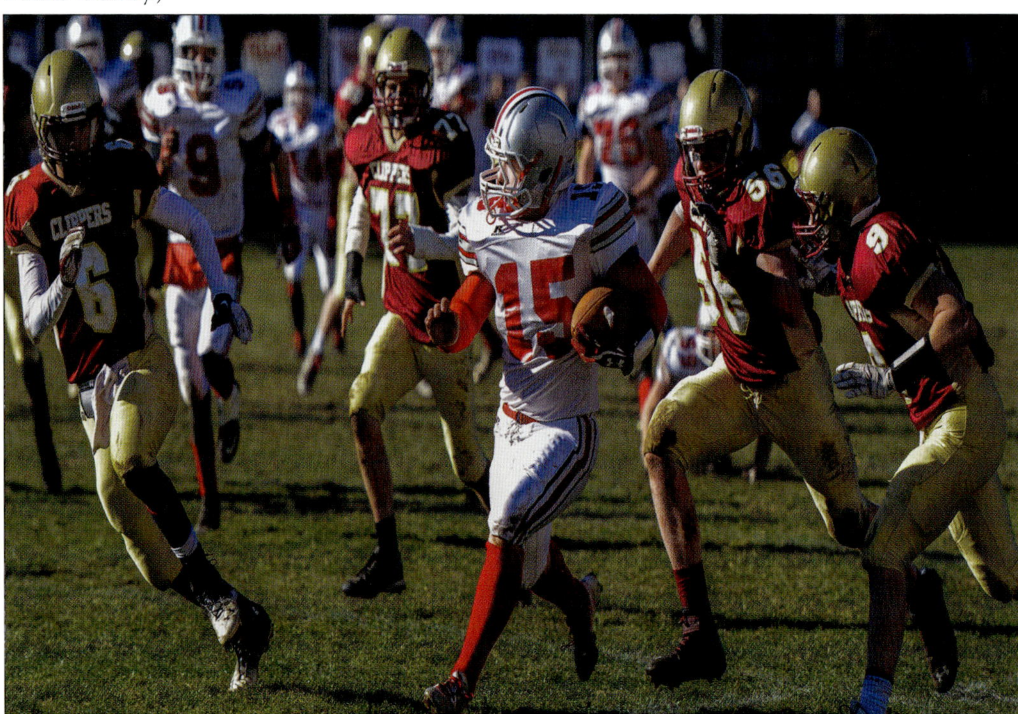

The big rivalry between Amesbury and Newburyport is never more evident than at the annual Thanksgiving Day football game. The stands are full with the crowd cheering on their hometown team. The players play their hearts out trying to become the victor. This rivalry has been going strong since 1891. (Photograph by Joey Walker.)

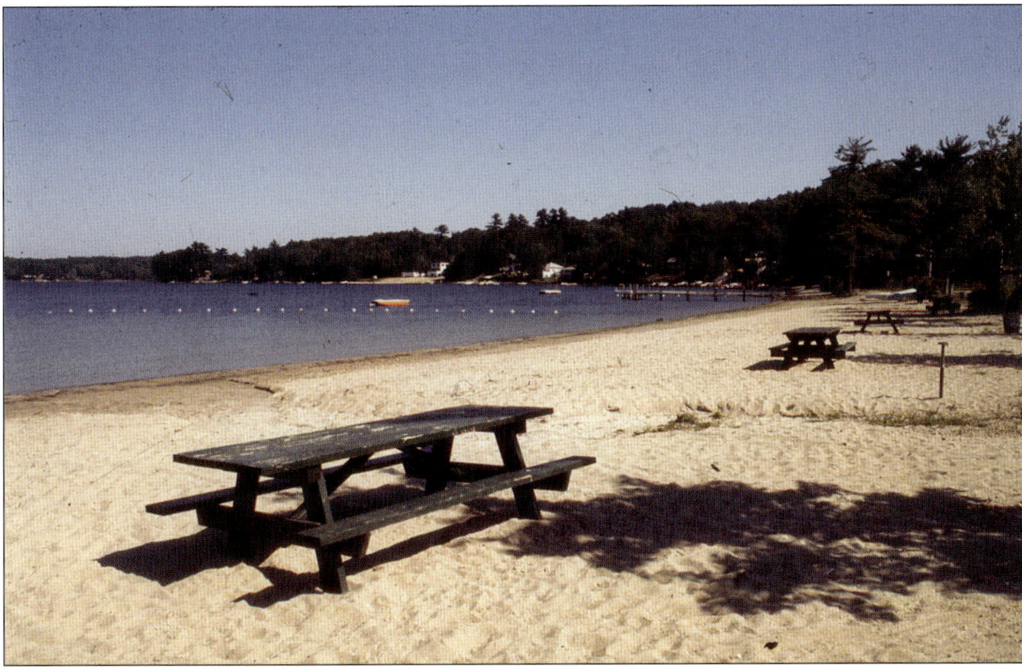

Lake Attitash borders Amesbury and Merrimac. Originally known as Kimball Pond, the name was changed to Lake Attitash in the late 1800s. People used to make their homes there seasonally, but now people live there year-round. Swimming and boating are popular lake pastimes. (Courtesy of the Amesbury Public Library.)

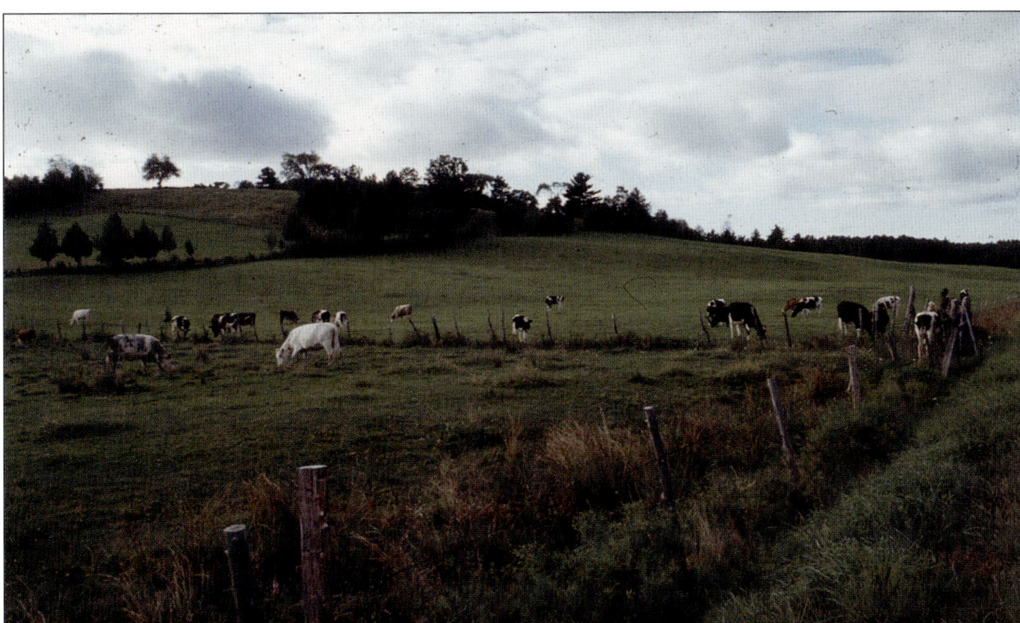

The 370-acre Woodsom Farm is surrounded by wetlands, woods, and marshes and bordered by the Powow River. It is great for hiking, walking, cross-country skiing, and biking. (Courtesy of the Amesbury Public Library.)

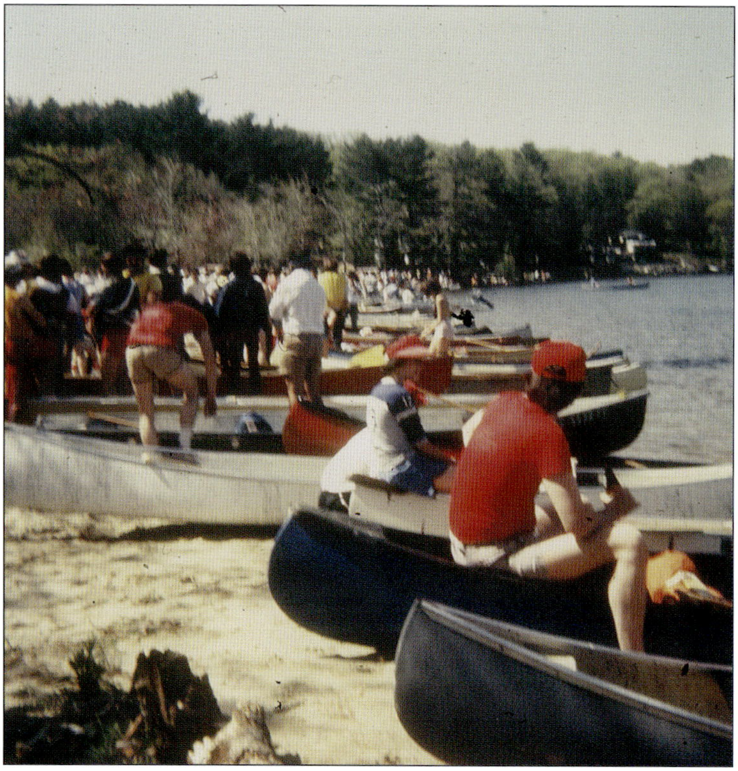

In 1980, the seventh annual Powow River Canoe race begin at the traditional starting line, at Sandy Beach on Lake Attitash, and followed the course through Meadowbrook to Tuxbury's Pond and the Powow River. It drew a record 228 paddling enthusiasts to the event. Spectators lined the banks of the Powow River to cheer on the record number of people that participated in the race. (Courtesy of the Amesbury Public Library.)

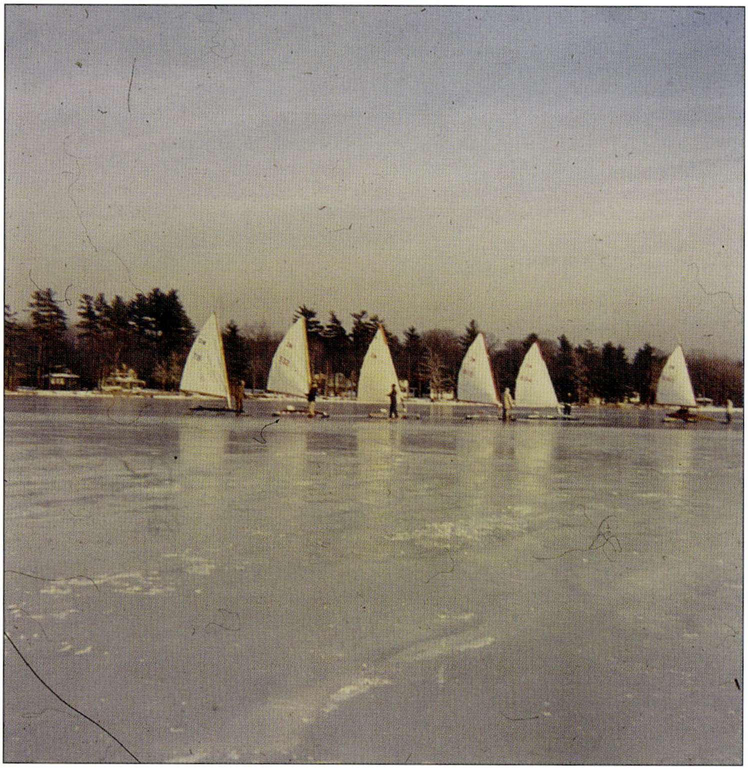

Ice boats on Lake Attitash were one of the most fun winter activities that people looked forward to. It was a popular activity for people that lived there. (Photograph by Betty Goodwin; courtesy of the Amesbury Public Library.)

In 1981, Leslie Goodwin sent money to a company in Michigan for a kit to construct his own ice boat, complete with sail. He built it so that he and his children, Paul and Julie, could enjoy ice boating on Lake Attitash during the winter. (Courtesy of Betty Goodwin and the Amesbury Public Library.)

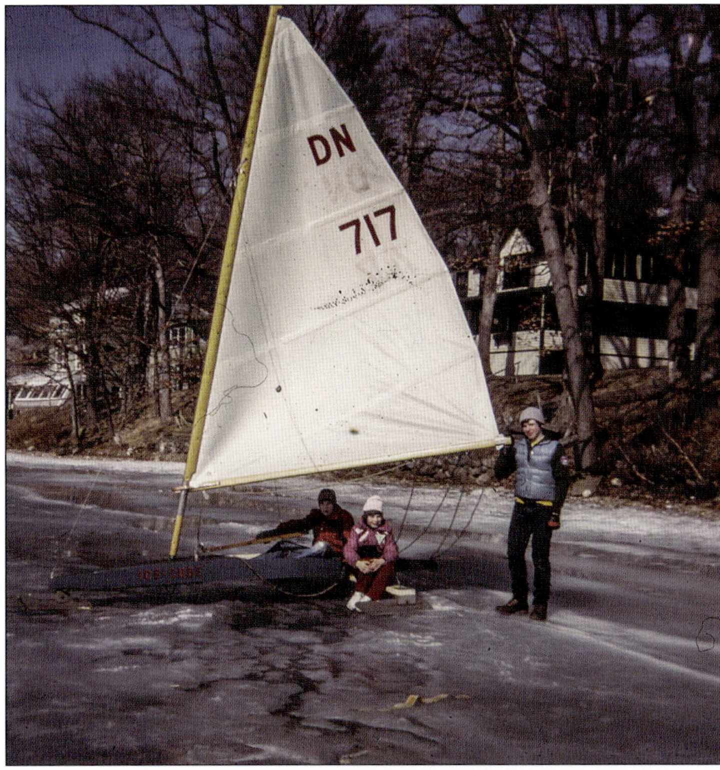

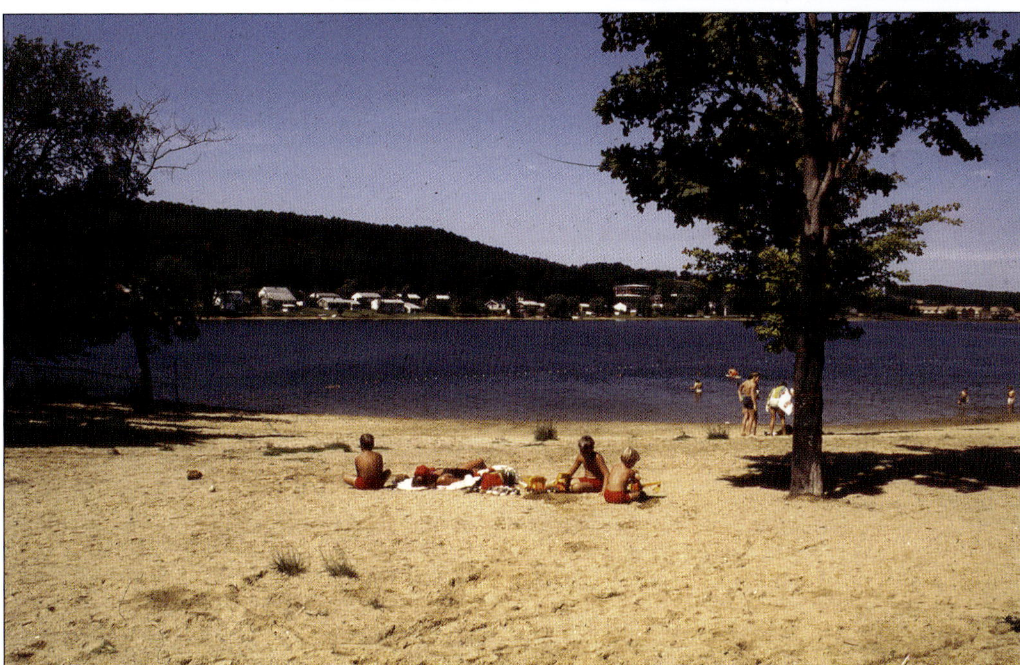

Lake Gardner was formed by the construction of a dam by the Salisbury Mills Corporation in 1872. In 1952, the lake was bought by the city. It was then that it started to be used by families. People enjoy fishing, boating, and swimming on the lake. (Courtesy of the Amesbury Public Library.)

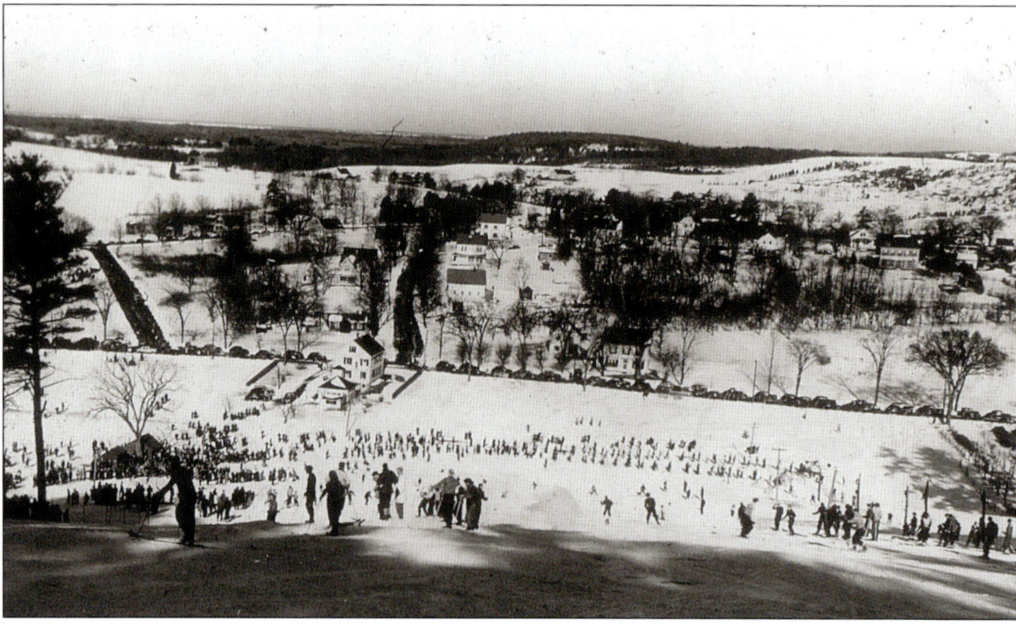

Locke's Hill is only half a mile from downtown Amesbury, and each winter, both novice and professional skiers would come to the hill. There were three tows and available instruction for beginners. In February 1980, Amesbury Ski Tow owner Donald Deschenes decided to make his own snow by installing a snow-making machine, to the delight of many skiers. (Courtesy of the Amesbury Public Library.)

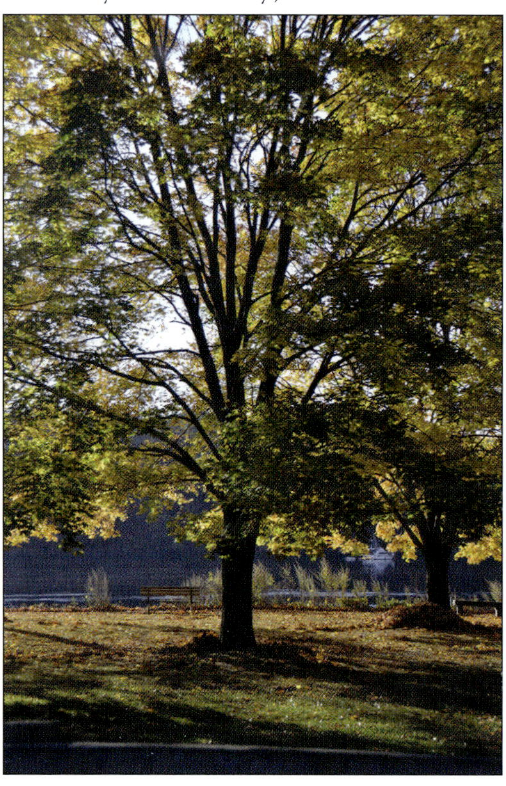

Alliance Park is located alongside the Merrimack River, where the frigate *Alliance* was launched in 1778. There are monuments in the park to the *Alliance* and local shipbuilders. The Amesbury Improvement Association is responsible for the park. (Photograph by the author.)

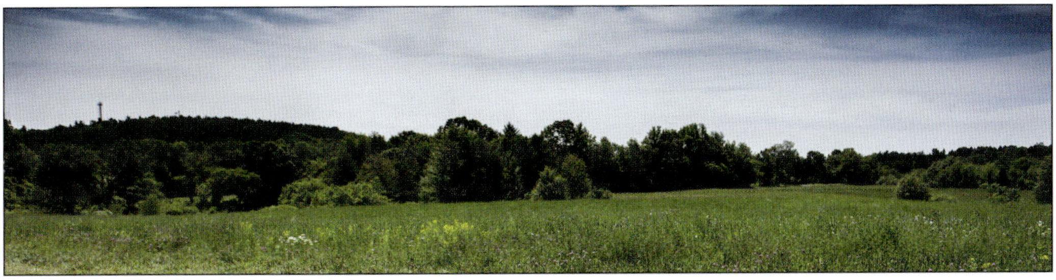

The Battis Farm is located on South Hampton Road and owned by the City of Amesbury. One can follow the trail down to Lake Gardner, and canoeing or kayaking is permitted. There is also a boardwalk to Lake Gardner Beach. (Photograph by Joey Walker.)

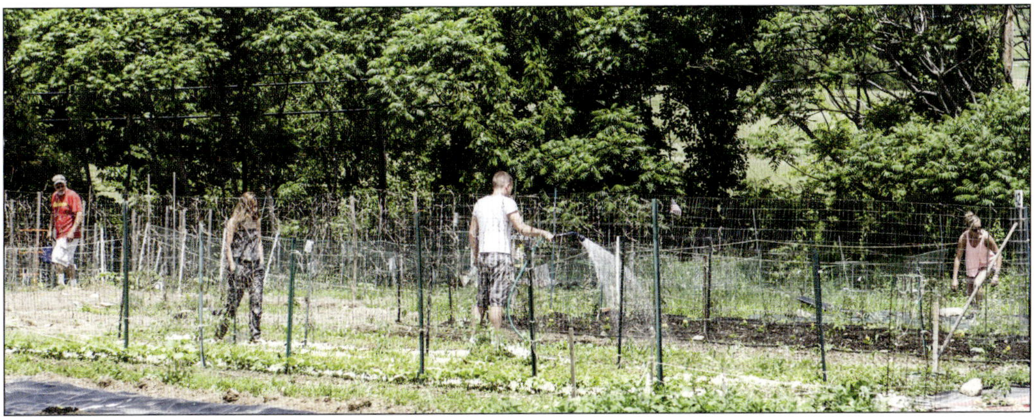

The community garden, owned by the City of Amesbury, is located in the Battis Farm on South Hampton Road. People can acquire their own plots for a fee. One will find the garden busy with people planting vegetables and flowers all summer long, as seen above in 2015. (Photograph by Joey Walker.)

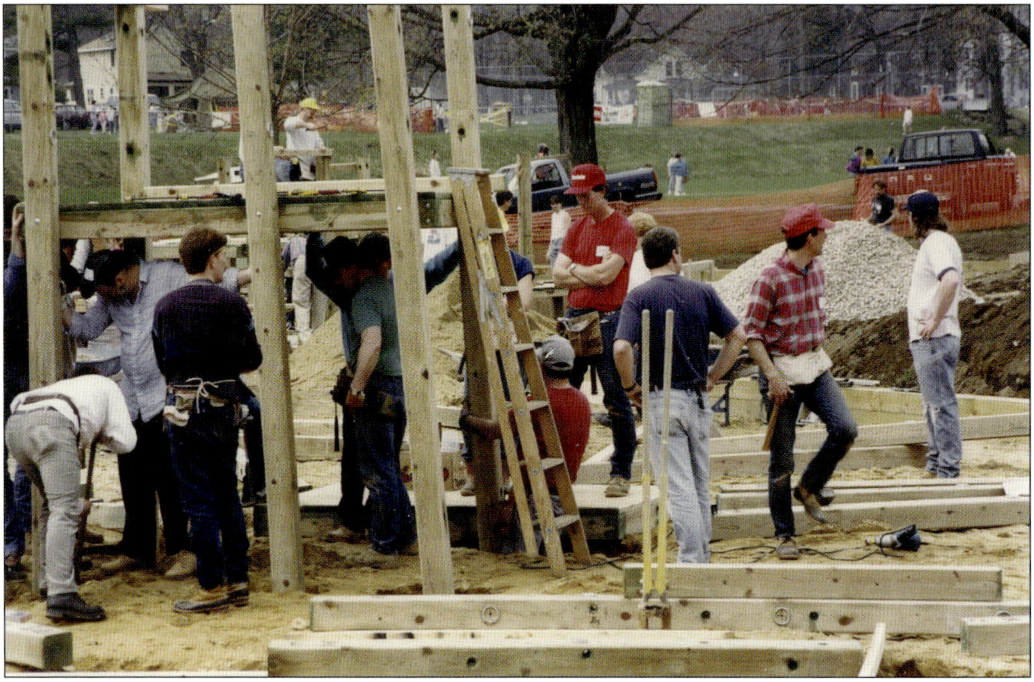

A group of dedicated parents, families, and residents of Amesbury had a dream of building a new playground at the town park for children. Committees were formed so that all aspects of the operation were covered. Through fundraising and contacting local businesses to donate their time, equipment, lumber, and money, their dream became a reality. For three weekends in May 1992, some 400 volunteers came to the park to help. There was a day care center set up so kids could come and play while their parents worked, and food was donated from local restaurants to feed the hungry volunteers. (Both, courtesy of Doug and Rose McBride.)

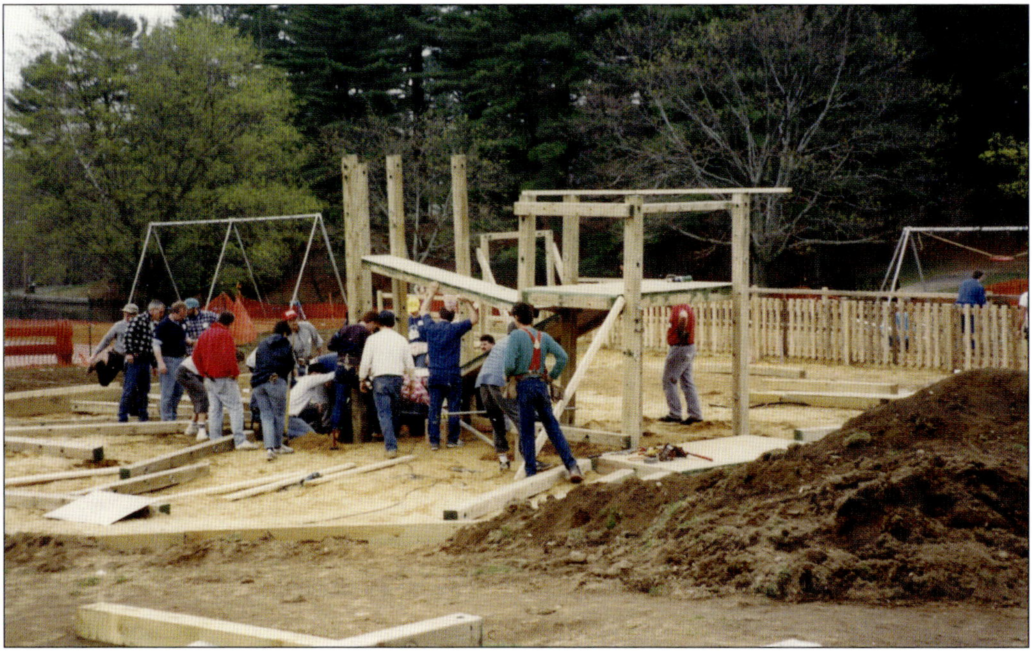

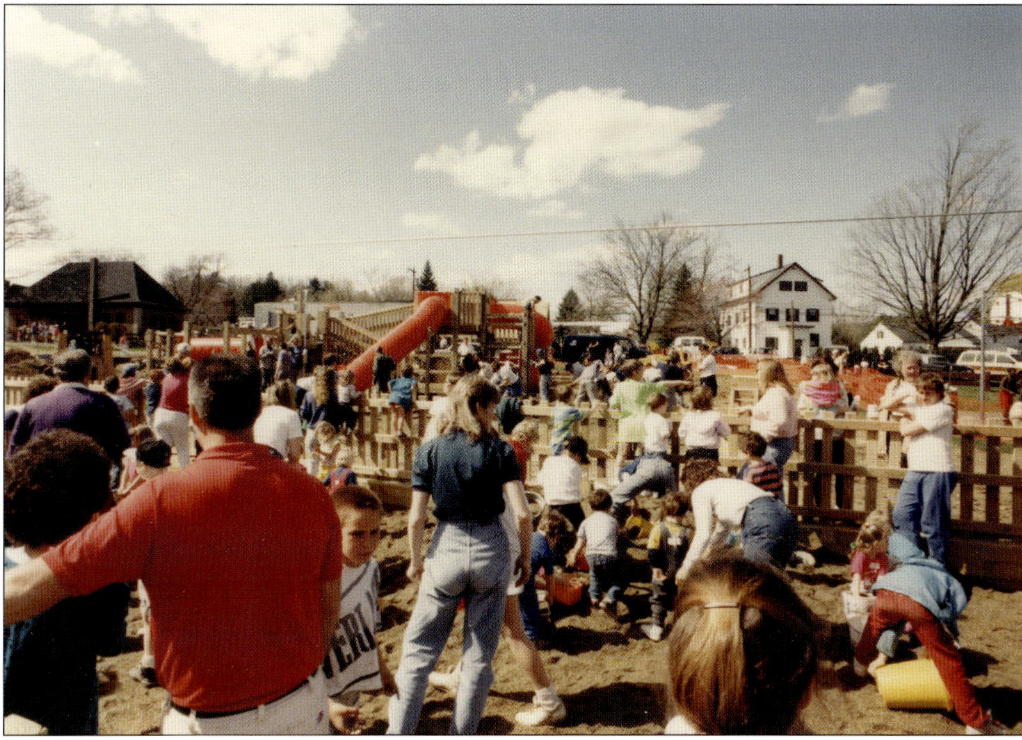

Children are playing while their parents and grandparents build them a new playground. These are the volunteers watching the kids. These children cannot wait to try out the new slides and swings but are having a great time playing in the sand. Bertha Shattler Ashby of Virginia donated $50,000 to the cause, and her family was there to dedicate the new park to the children of Amesbury. The dedication ceremony took place in May 1992, and there is a stone at the park in her memory. (Both, courtesy of Doug and Rose McBride.)

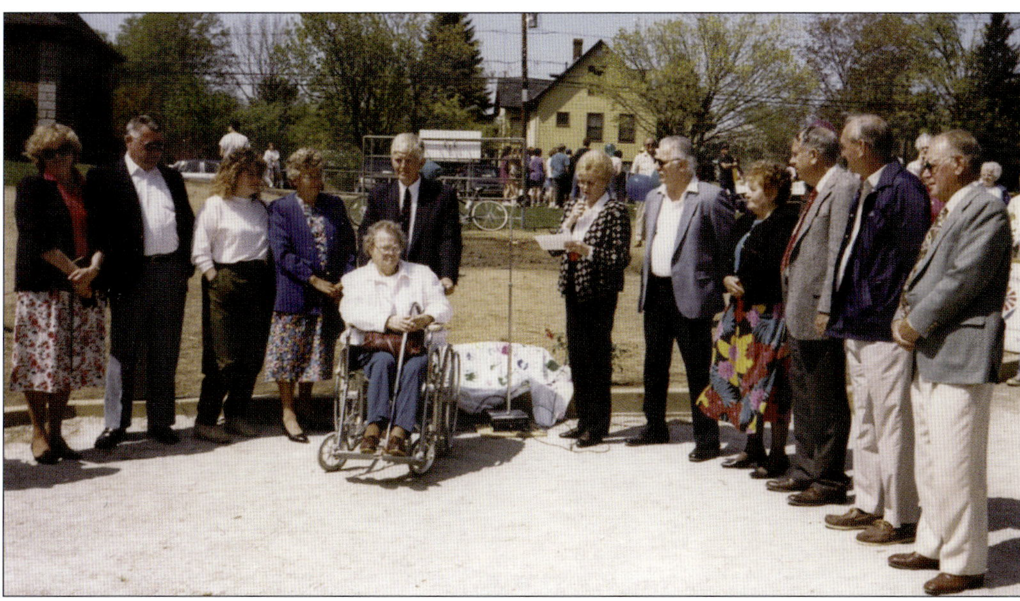

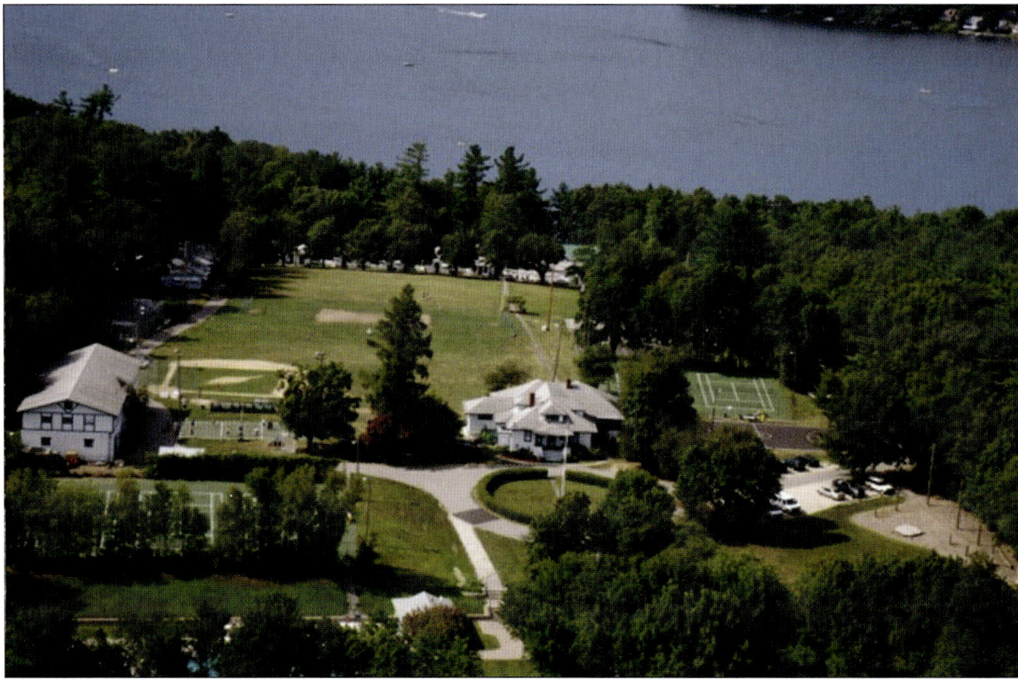

Camp Bauercrest is a traditional overnight sports camp for boys that has been delivering unforgettable summers since 1931. Bauercrest is a brotherhood forged through healthy competition and camaraderie to create an experience where boys make friends, learn new skills, and gain experiences that truly last for a lifetime. The camp's goal is to build a boy's identity and self-esteem through the values of sportsmanship, teamwork, achievement, and responsibility. (Both, photograph by Eric Rightor; courtesy of Camp Bauercrest.)

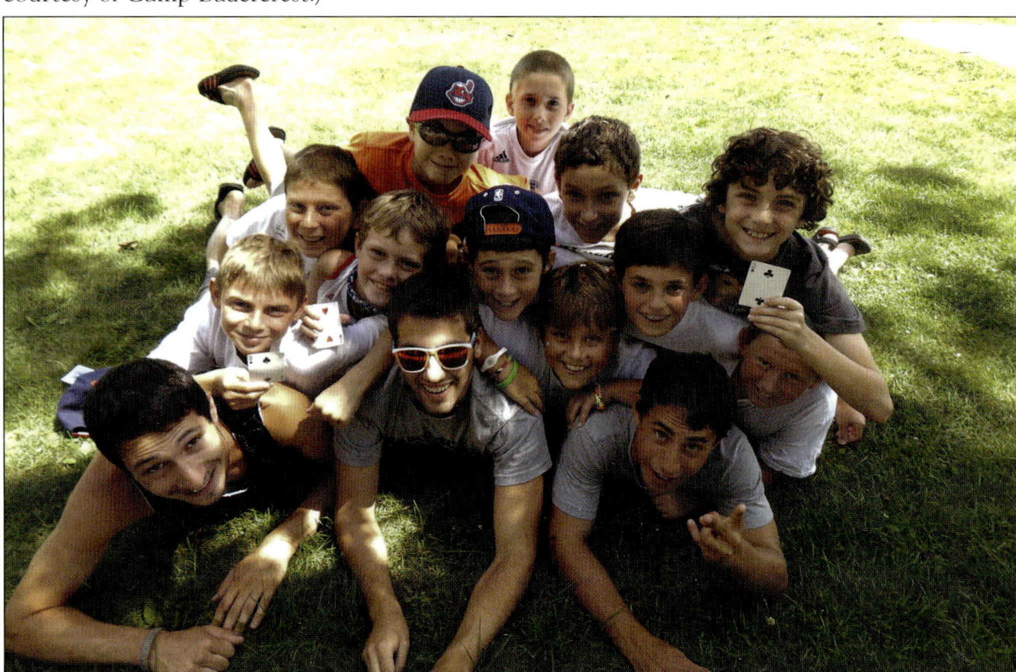

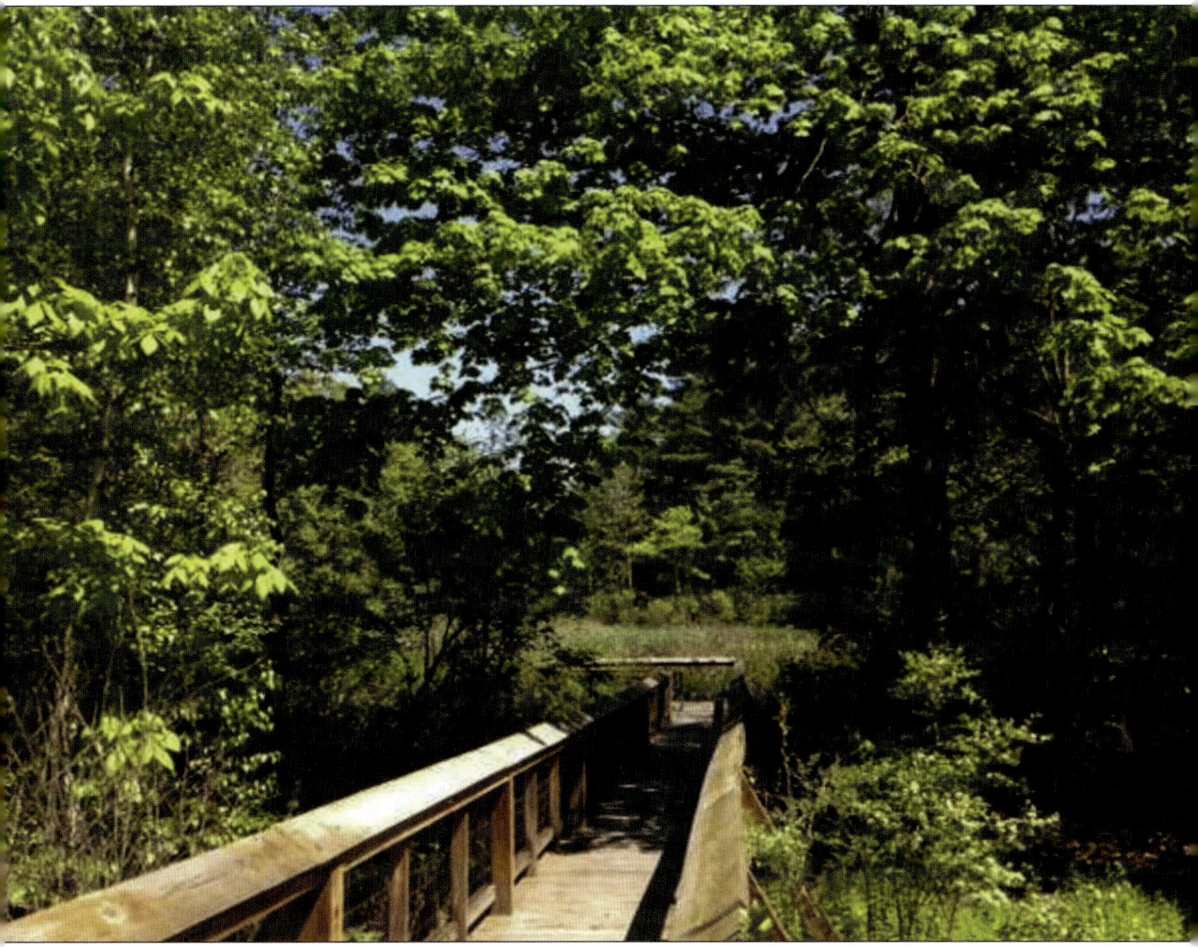

The Camp Kent Nature Center is on 17 acres of conservation land established by the City of Amesbury in 1997. The property, formerly a Girl Scout camp, has a main lodge, a smaller lodge used as a classroom, a boathouse, a workshop, bathrooms, and a changing room. The camp is connected to the Powow River and Lake Gardner. This area has a variety of habitats, including vernal wetlands, marshes, meadows, and the forest along the Powow River and Lake Gardner. More than 100 bird species, a variety of reptiles and amphibians, fox, coyote, and deer make this preserve their home. Camp Kent's summer program includes archery and sailing. The goal is a year-round nature center whose purpose is conservation, education, and recreation, with birding programs, live animal presentations, a butterfly garden, a 4,000-square-foot wildflower garden, a trail created by Eagle Scouts, and a volunteer group that meets monthly to maintain the landscape and programs. (Courtesy of R.J. Knecht, Camp Kent.)

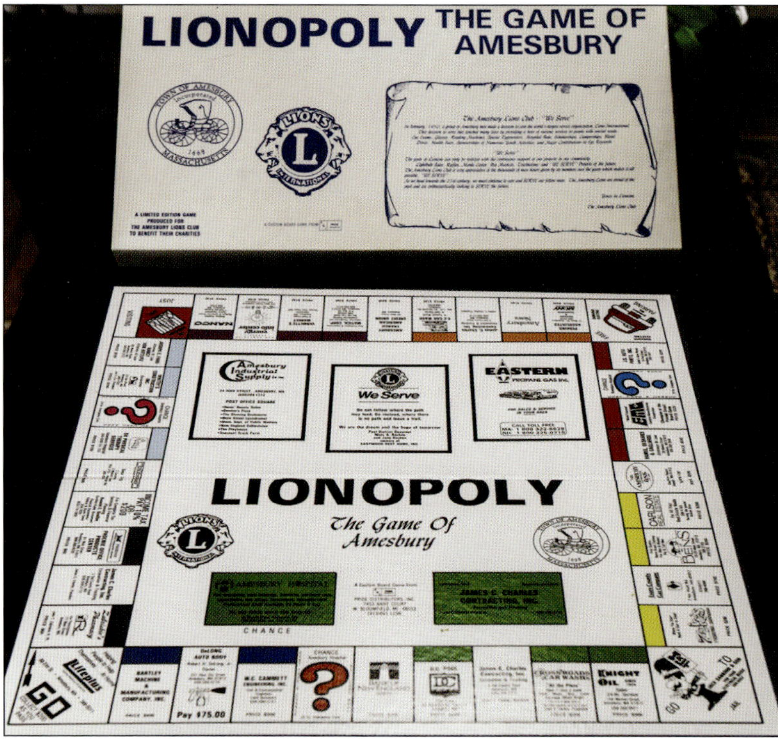

The Amesbury Lions Club had a Lionopoly game made. Names of local businesses and industries have replaced the names that are on the original game. Proceeds from the sale of the game went to local charities, the Massachusetts Eye Research Foundation, and scholarships that the Amesbury Lions award annually. (Photograph by Joey Walker; courtesy of Steve Deorocki and Normand Pare.)

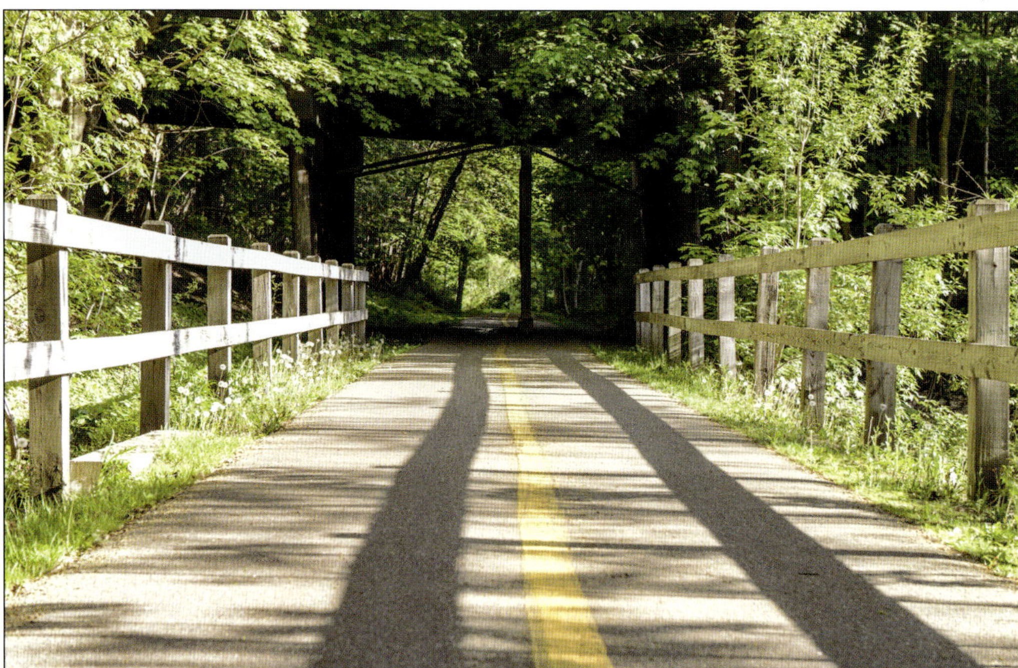

The Riverwalk is part of the trails that run through Amesbury, Salisbury, Newburyport, and Newbury. The Riverwalk is along the Powow River, which joins the Merrimack River. One can walk, bicycle, and rollerblade along the trail, which is home to a variety of plants and animals. (Photograph by Joey Walker.)

Four

CHURCHES AND SCHOOLS

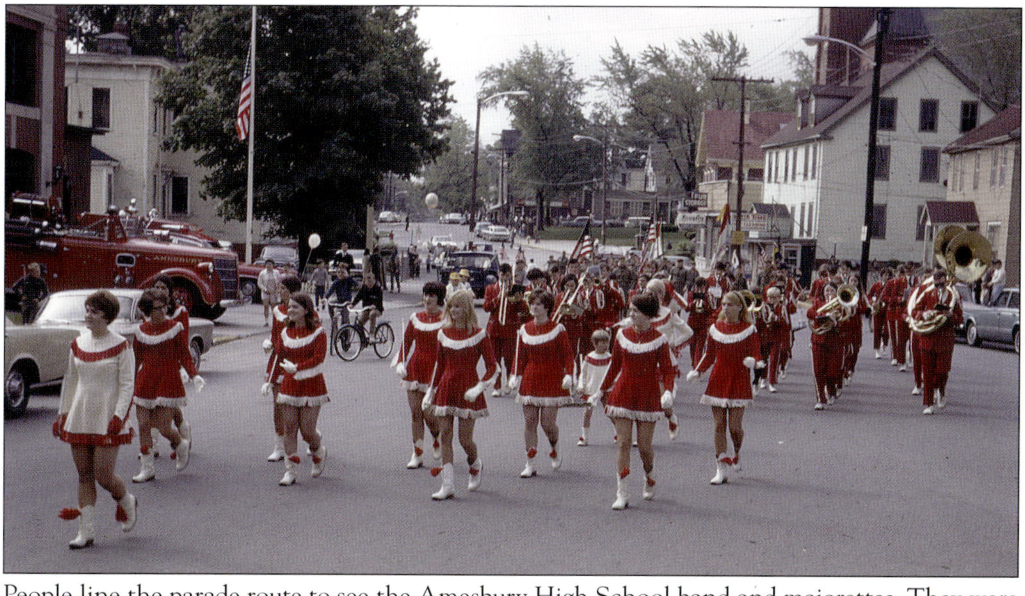

People line the parade route to see the Amesbury High School band and majorettes. They were available to play and perform for various sporting events, Memorial Day, Veterans Day, and Santa parades to entertain the crowds. (Courtesy of the Amesbury Public Library.)

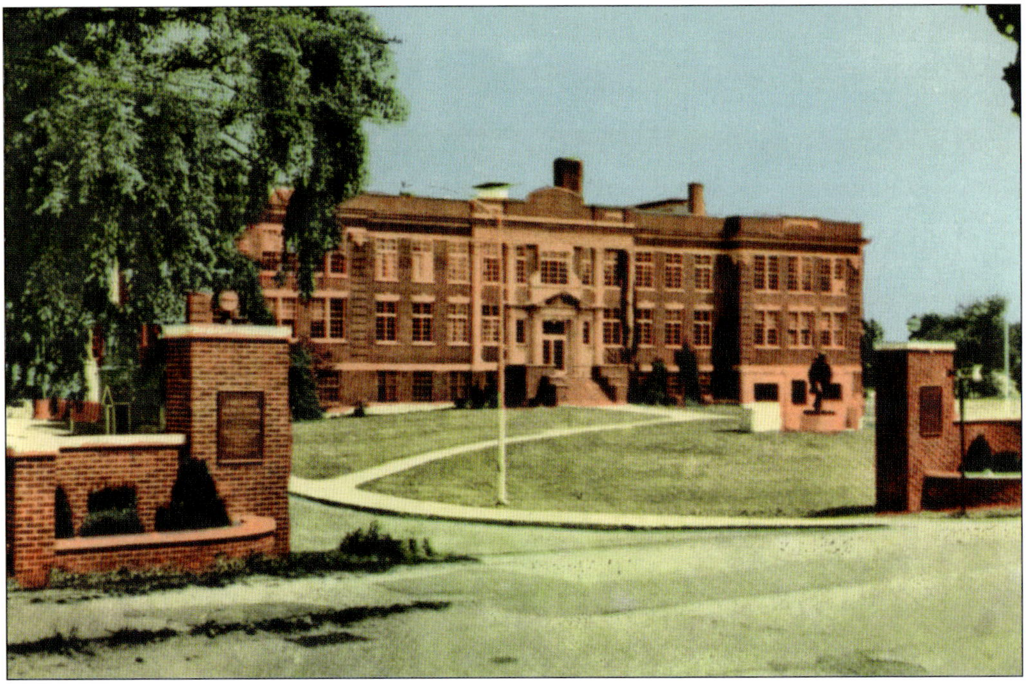

Amesbury High School was built in 1917. In April 1964, firefighters battled this fierce blaze, which started while classes were in session. Miraculously, no one was injured. The school was destroyed, and students had to go to Haverhill High School. The new high school opened in 1968. (Above, courtesy of Ron Gagnon; below, courtesy of the Amesbury Public Library.)

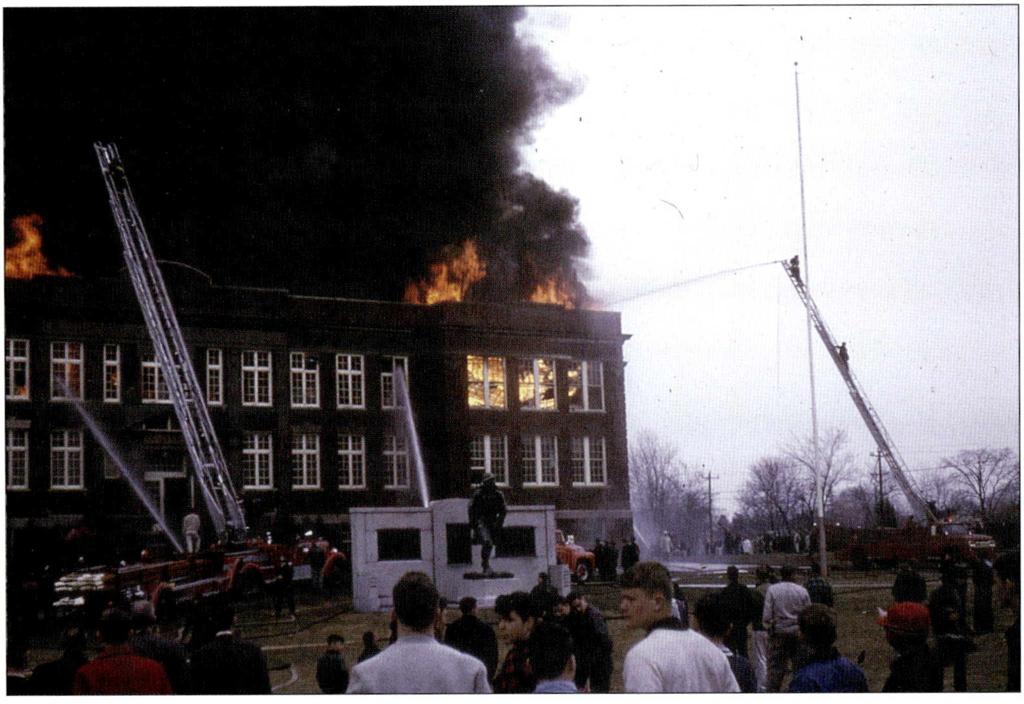

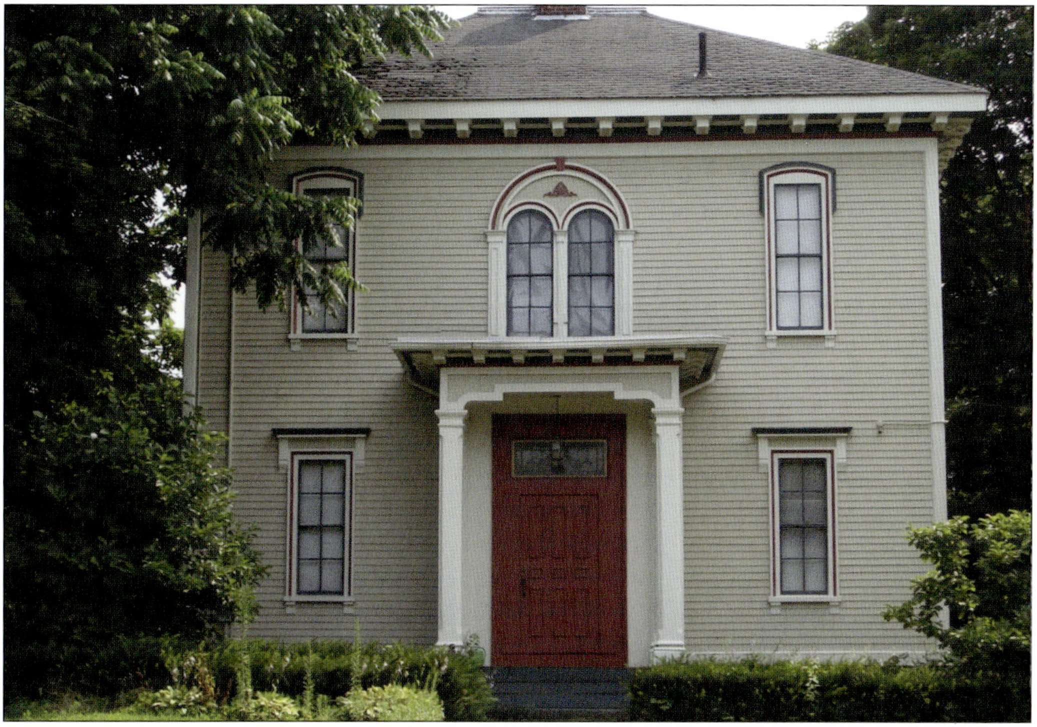

In 1870, the Bartlett School was built, and in 1922, the school went from two rooms to four. The school closed in 1968. The Bartlett Museum was opened in 1968 for the 300th anniversary of the founding of the city. (Courtesy of Dianne Cole.)

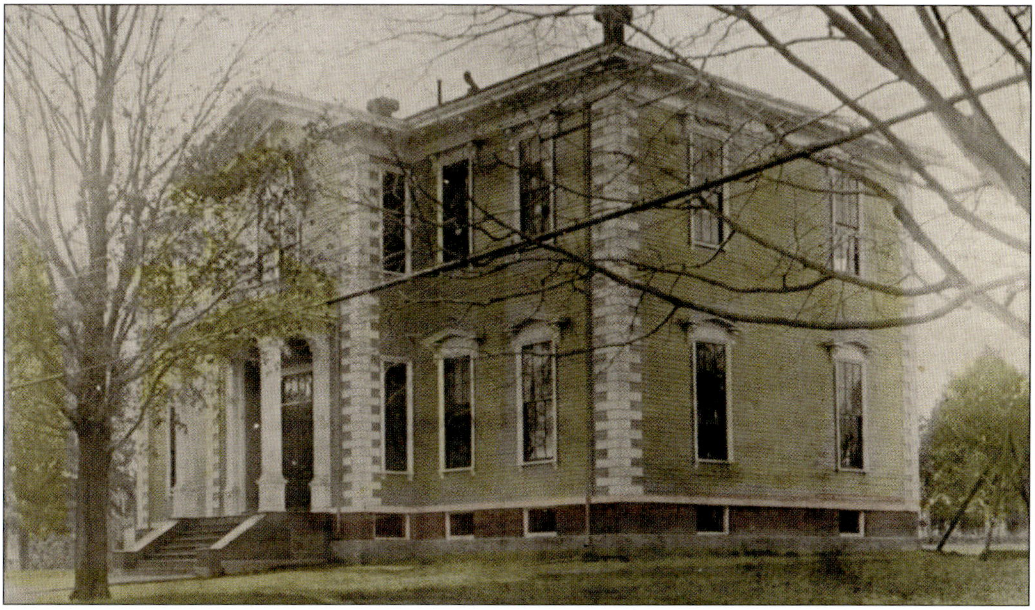

The Whittier/Prospect School was built in Salisbury Village in 1872. In July 1876, a class of seven graduated, and in 1917, the school changed its name to Prospect School. In 1936, it was changed back to Whittier. The school became apartment buildings in 1985. (Courtesy of the Amesbury Public Library and Tom Hanshaw.)

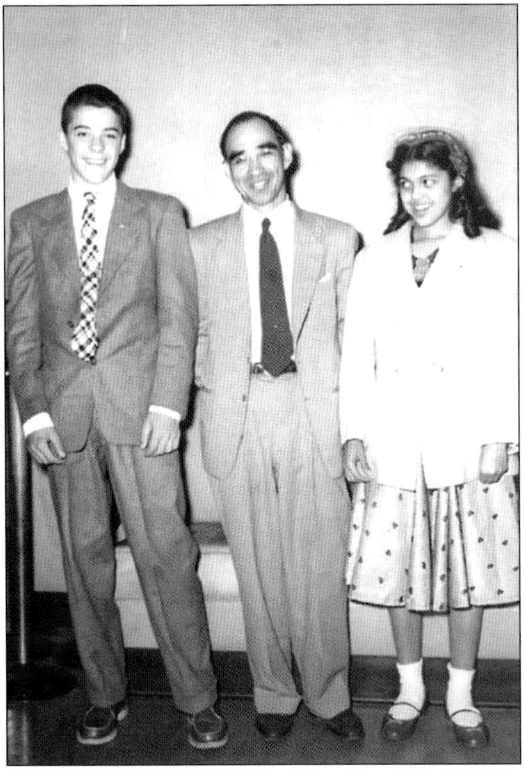

Edward Boulter, principal at Amesbury Junior High School, received a letter from Yasuo Ishii, a teacher in the Heda Secondary School in Shizuola, Japan, inquiring if Amesbury students would like to correspond with Japanese schoolchildren. The students from both countries sent paintings, social studies papers, and letters. Ishii was saving money to buy a typewriter to use in the school. Boulter contacted Remington Rand Company in New York to see if the company would ship a typewriter to the Heda School if money could be raised. The company agreed, and it would be built in Japan. The typewriter was delivered to Tokyo with American parts by Japanese workers. An invitation was sent to appear on the *Home Television Show* with Hugh Downs to talk about the program with the students. On May 12, 1954, Betty Ann Sanford and Walter Brown went to New York along with Boulter, and they told the story of the project. The students were met by the Japanese consul general Jun Tsuchiya. (Both, courtesy of the Amesbury Public Library.)

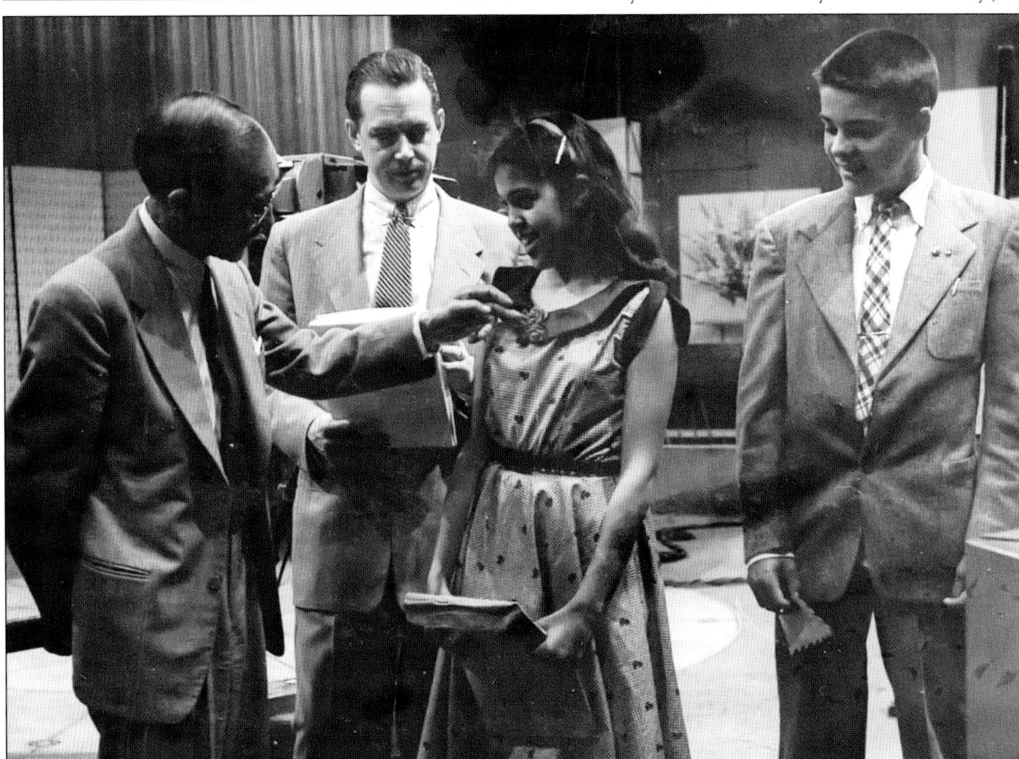

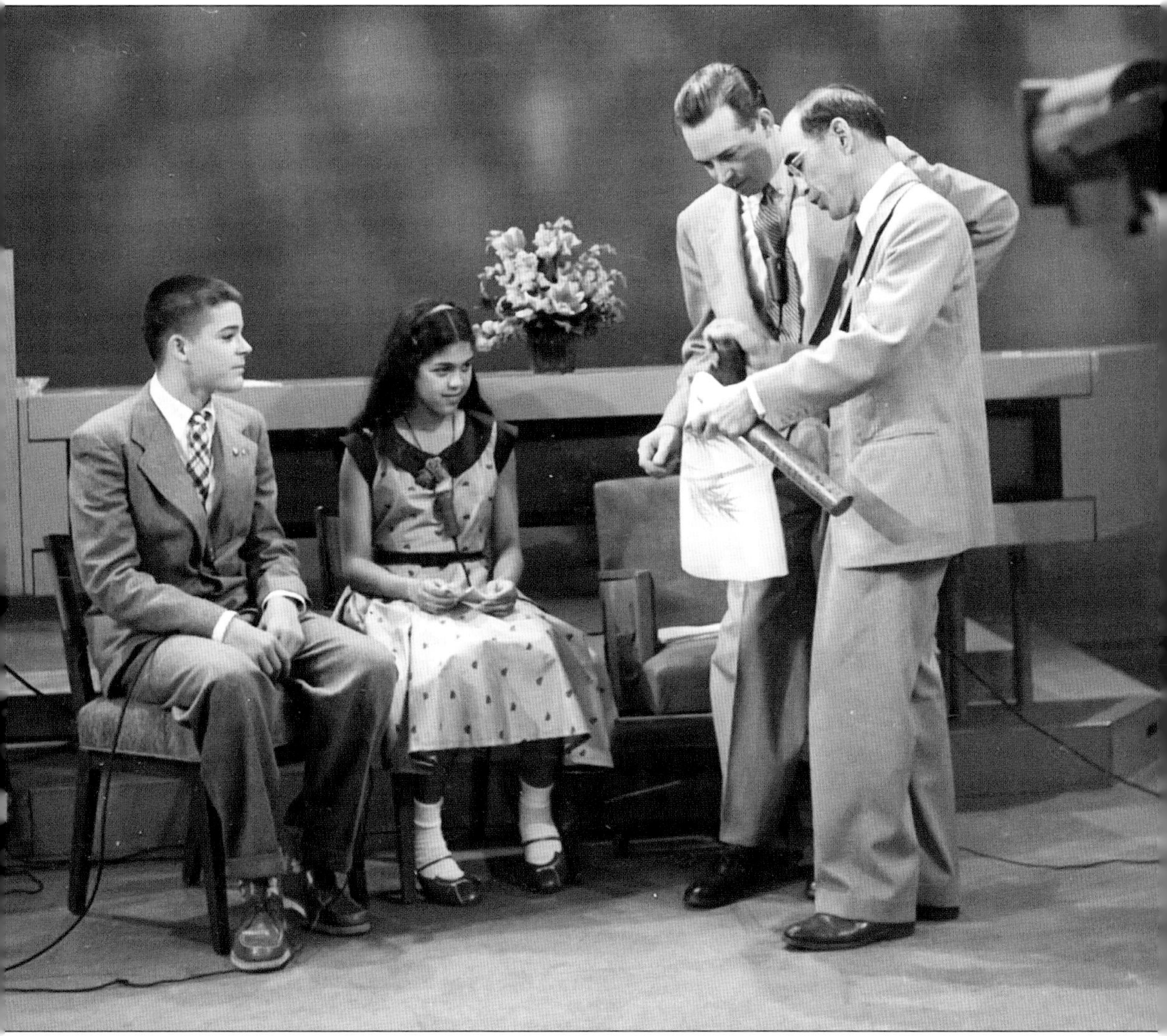

Pictured here in 1955 are, from left to right, Walter Brown, Betty Ann Sanford, Hugh Downs (the announcer of the television show), and Jun Tsuchiya, the Japanese consul. In recognition for helping the Japanese students and teacher get the typewriter that they needed, Consul Tsuchiya is presenting a hand-painted scroll of Mount Fuji for the students to take back to Amesbury Junior High School. (Courtesy of the Amesbury Public Library.)

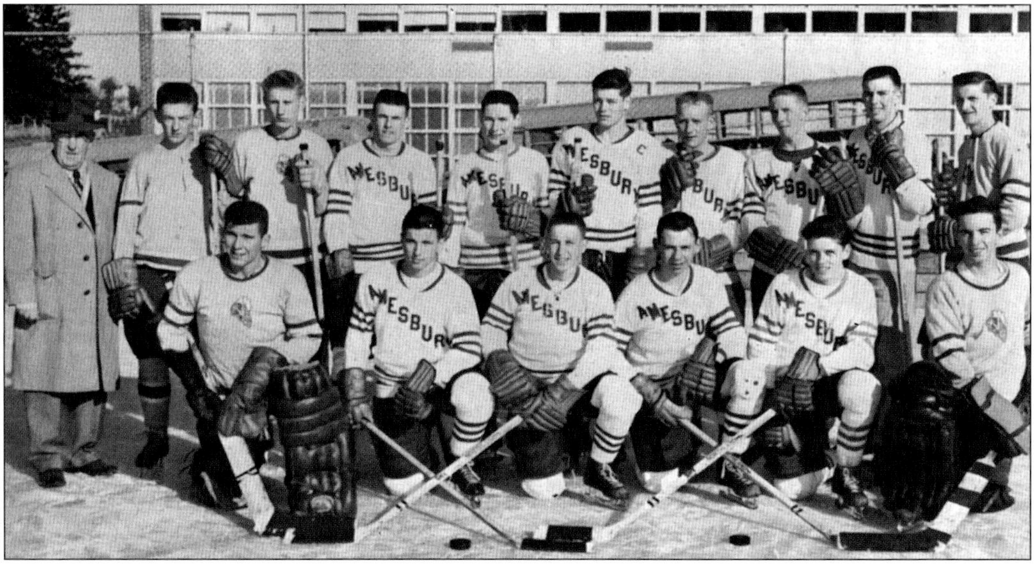

The 1957 Amesbury High School Hockey team went on to the finals. Pictured here are, from left to right, (first row) Carl Orkney, Stan Andrews, Carl Mitchell, Leo Dupre, Norm Parent, and Bob Cook; (second row) Coach Roy, T. Houlihan, Frank Briggs, Robert Martin, Bill Morin, Captain Cressy, Don Roy, Bill Cote, Dick Watkins, and Ken Terry. Leo Dupre and Don Roy were selected for the annual North Shore Allstar Game. Leo Dupre played a major role in both Allstar wins. (Courtesy of Dianne Cole.)

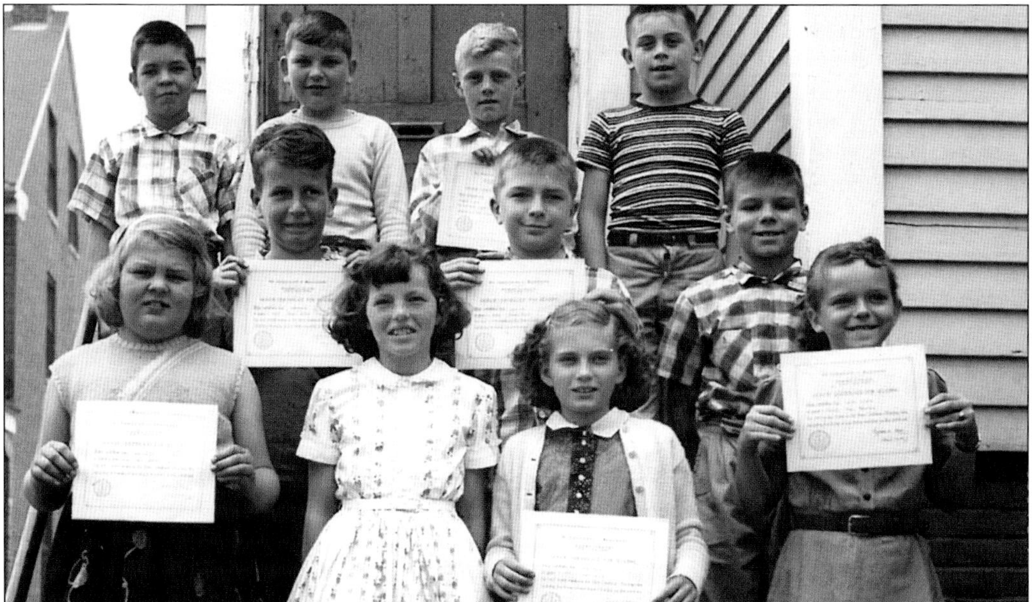

The Ordway School's fourth grade students participated in the Amesbury Public Library Summer Reading Program in the summer of 1957. The students received an honor certificate signifying that they read and reported on 20 books. Pictured here are, from left to right, (first row) Linda Titcomb, Carol White, Johnina Genova, and Linda Lizotte; (second row) Thomas Garrett, Daniel Cote, and Richard Poulin; (third row) Richard Reifke, Brian Paine, Albert Shaw, and Clifford Smith. (Courtesy of the Amesbury Public Library.)

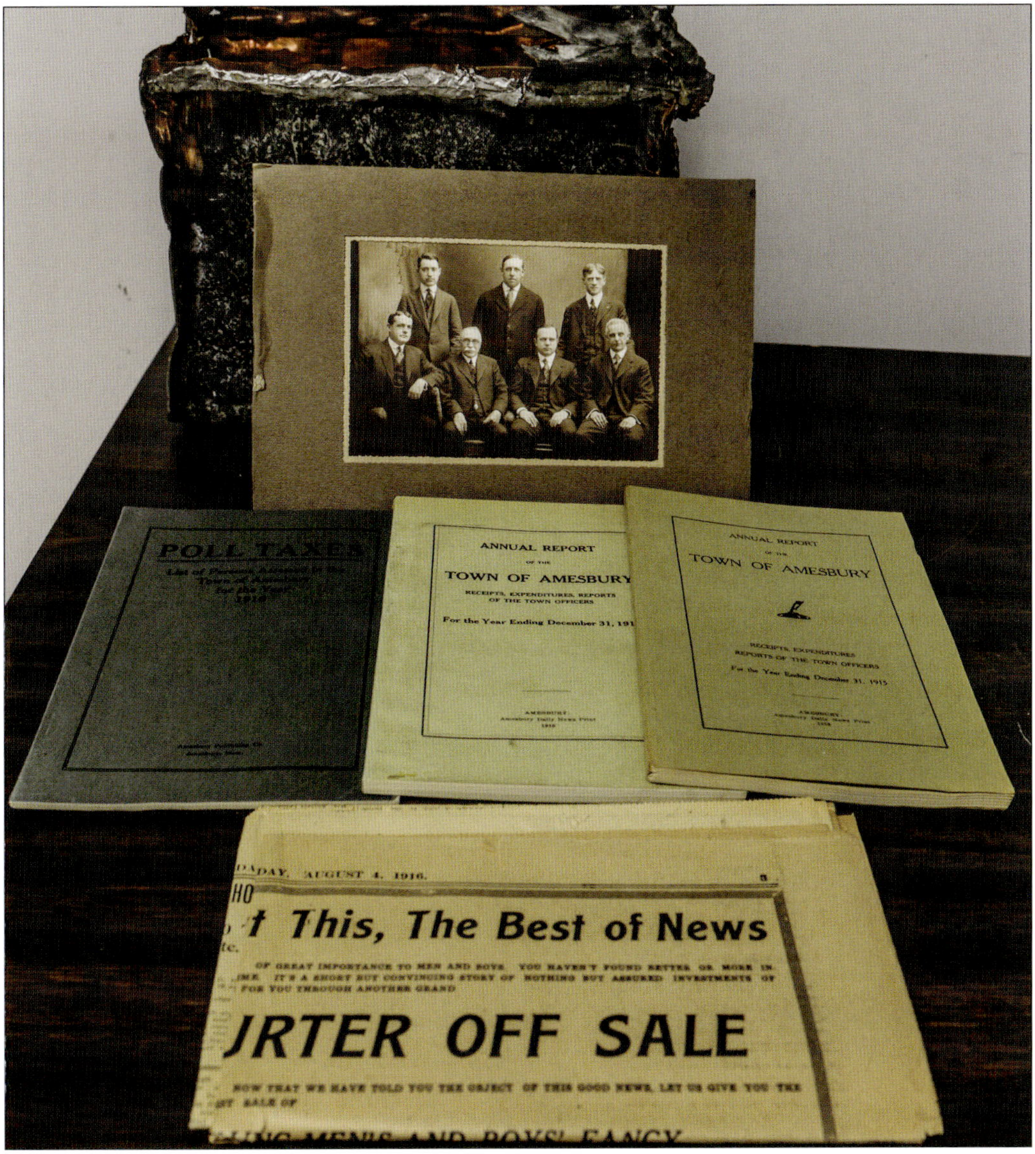

In 1917, a time capsule was placed in the cornerstone of Amesbury High School. The school was destroyed by a fire in 1964, and the time capsule was found but stored away. Firefighters doing work in the town annex stumbled upon the capsule in 1994. The capsule contained photographs of school officials; town reports; copies of the newspaper; coins; postage stamps; photographs of Market Square; the automobile business section of town; views from Whittier Hill; a letter written by Edward Brown, a genealogist, in which he left instructions in verse on how to open the box; and signatures of students and faculty. It was truly amazing that this capsule was even found due to the fire. The firefighters were in awe of what they found and amazed at the condition of the materials. (Photograph by Joey Walker.)

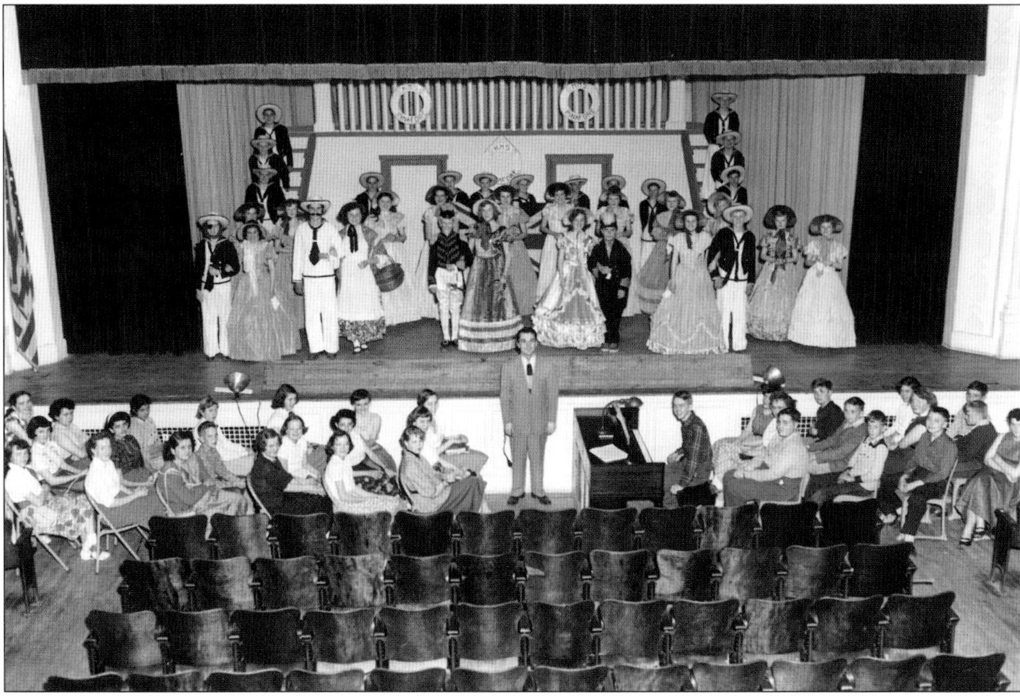

Amesbury Junior High School presented the play *H.M.S. Pinafore* on May 8, 1954. Pictured here are the cast and chorus of the play. Alphonse Tatarunis was the director of the play and chorus. (Courtesy of the Amesbury Public Library.)

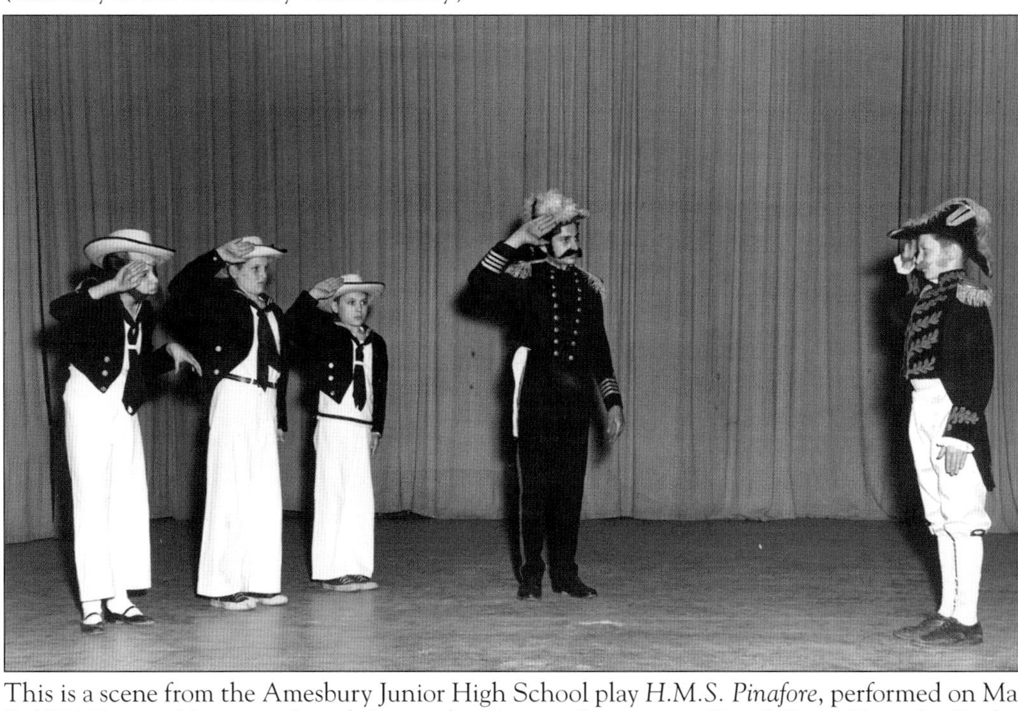

This is a scene from the Amesbury Junior High School play *H.M.S. Pinafore*, performed on May 8, 1954. Pictured here are, from left to right, Patricia Stromquist, David Terry, Timothy Hodge, Peter Kokaras, and Randolph Morse. (Courtesy of the Amesbury Public Library.)

Holy Family Parish of Amesbury celebrated its 15th anniversary with a liturgy and a family carnival and barbecue. Eight-year-old Ava Garvey was the lucky winner of the ice-cream eating contest. She had a lot of competition and came out victorious. (Photograph by Joey Walker.)

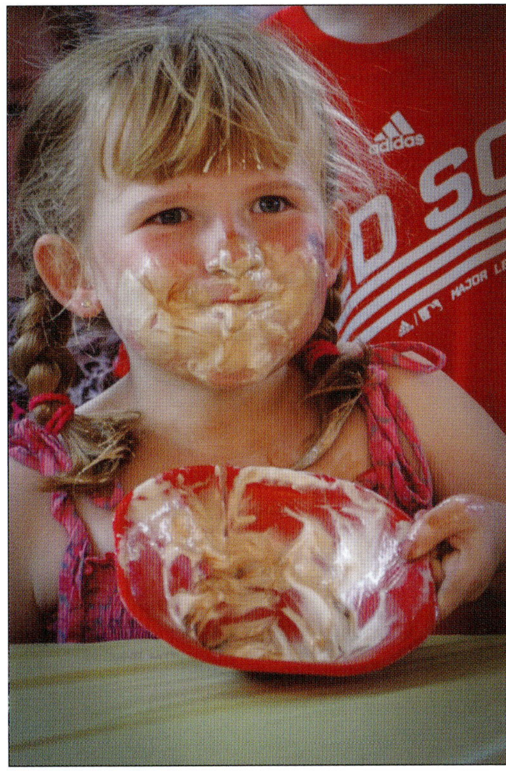

St. Joseph's Church reached their 100th anniversary in 1966. Rev. John Brady encouraged the people of Amesbury to get a church of their own, and once the church was established, they added on so that they could have a school. In May 1998, St. Joseph's and Sacred Heart Church became Holy Family Parish. (Courtesy of the Amesbury Public Library.)

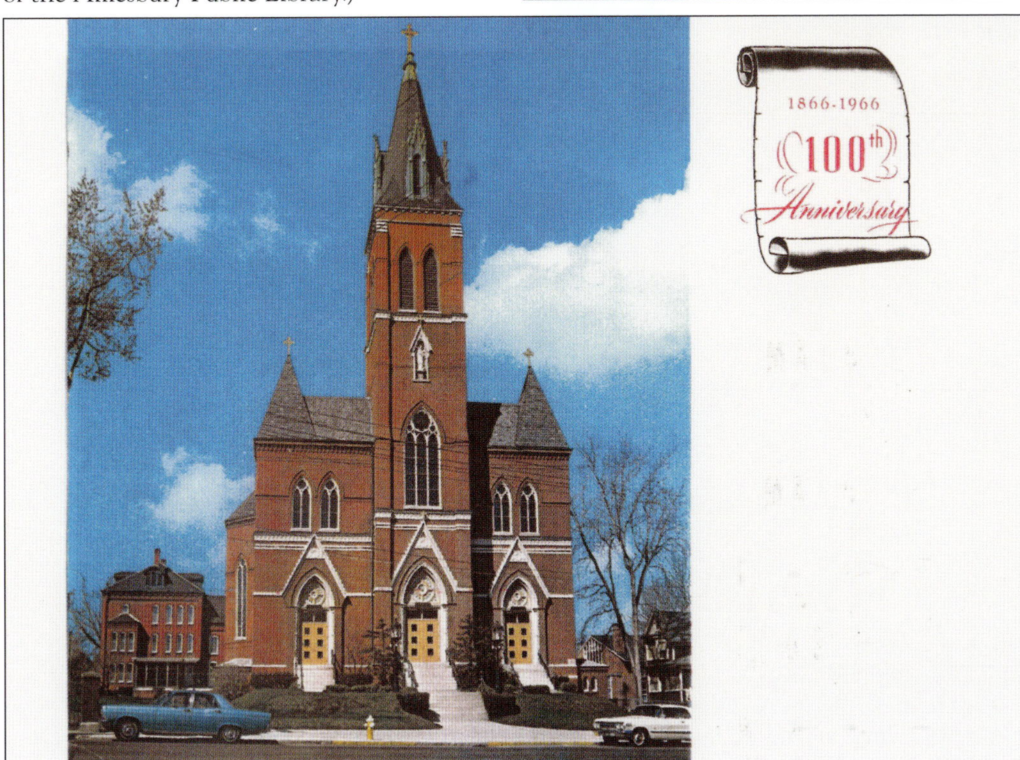

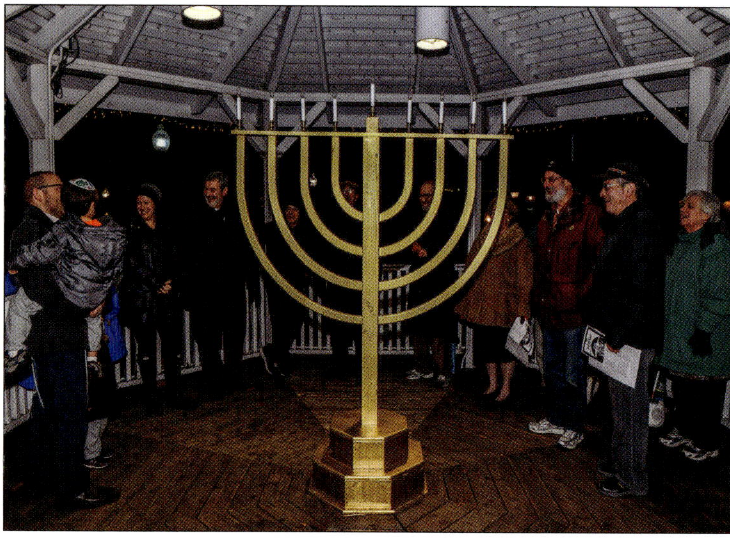

Rabbi Avi Poupko of Congregation Ahavas Achim in Newburyport led a first-ever lighting of a menorah at the Amesbury gazebo in December 2013. On the first night, one light is lit, and on every successive night, an additional light is added so that on the eighth night, eight lights are lit. It was arranged by Amesbury resident Rachel Barcelona. (Photograph by Joey Walker.)

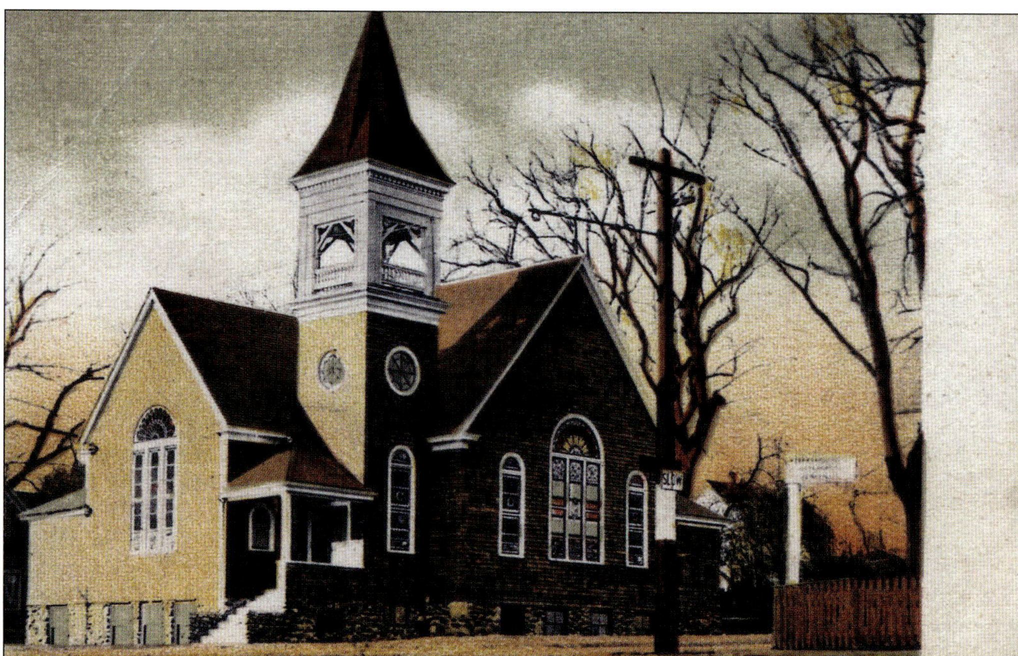

Point Shore Christian Church was also known as Grace Church. It is in what was once Salisbury Point but now is called the Point Shore area of Amesbury. The church was constructed in 1905 for a congregation that has historical significance. The original Christian Church was organized in 1820 with 32 members. They met at various places until a meetinghouse was built in 1827. They outgrew the meetinghouse and built this structure. It is now a private residence. (Courtesy of Ron Gagnon and Amesbury Public Library.)

St. James Church was damaged in a fire in 1899 when the opera house burned down, and downtown was in ruins. In 1903, the current St. James Church was built. The church suffered another fire in 2001, but it was able to repair the damage. In 2007, they were able to add a play area, nursery, and toddler room. (Photograph by the author.)

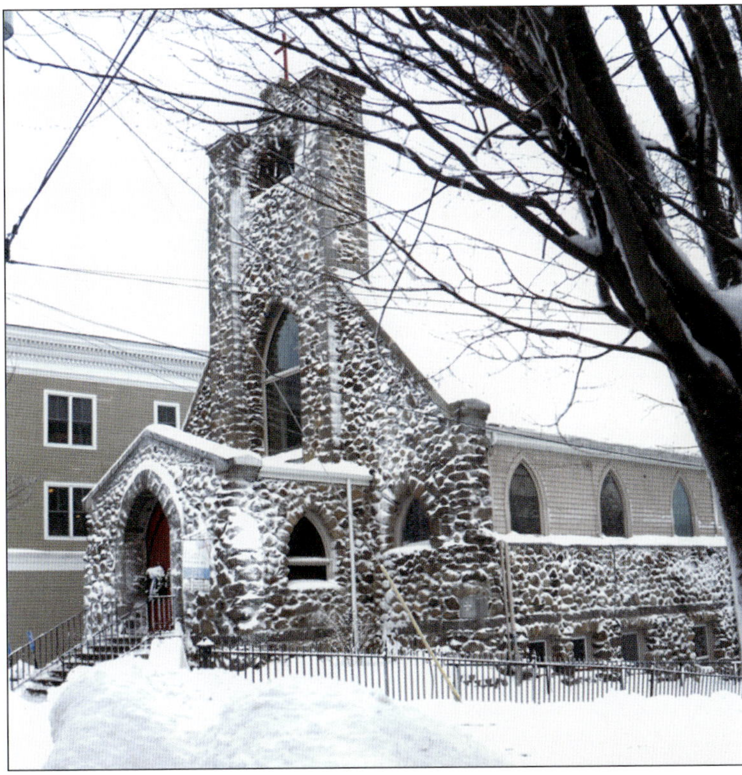

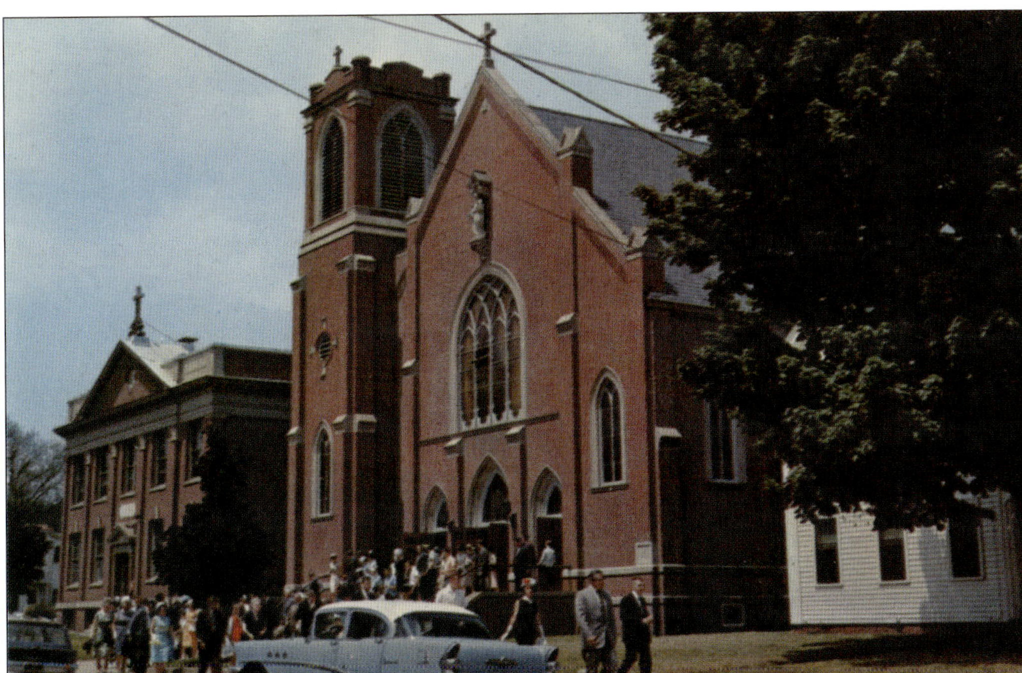

The service has ended at Sacred Heart Church. Note all of the fashionable women wearing gloves and hats. They are all wearing dresses, and men are in suits and ties. (Courtesy of the Amesbury Public Library.)

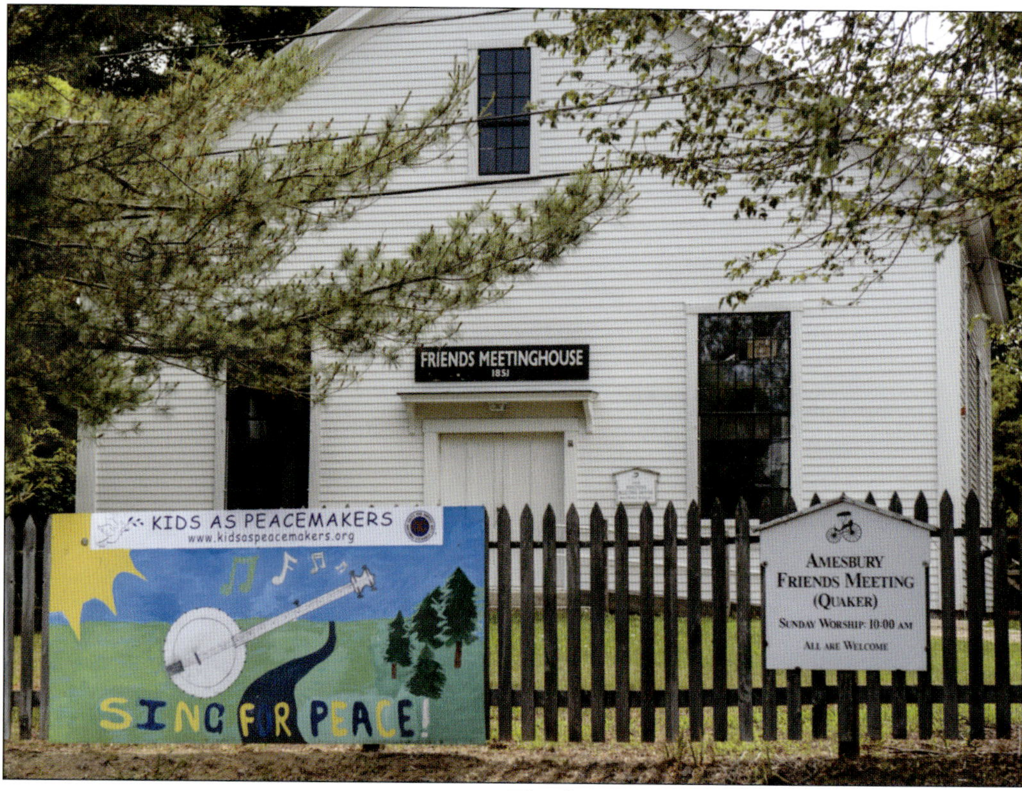

The first worship service in Amesbury was held in 1705. The Friends meetinghouse on Friend Street was built in 1851. John Greenleaf Whittier, the famous poet, was on the building committee for this meetinghouse. In 2015, the Friends continue to meet on Sundays. The meetinghouse is open to everyone in the community to use for community events. On display is a mural made by the children. (Photograph by Joey Walker.)

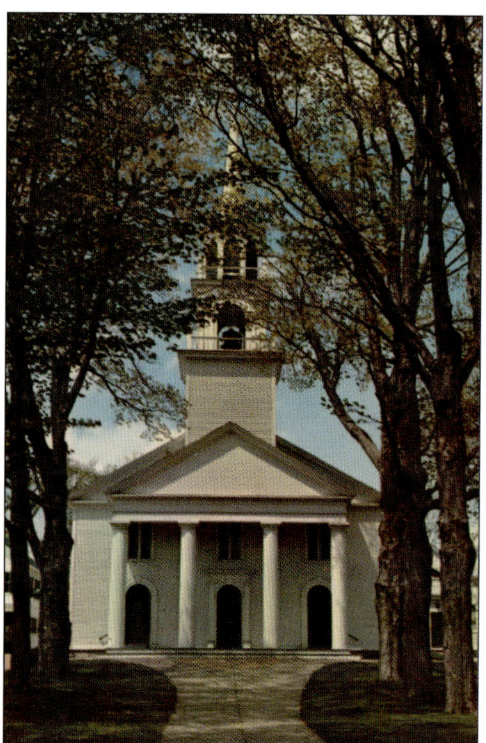

In 1832, it was known as the Unitarian Congregational Society. In 1887, the name was changed to Main Street Congregational Church. The church has a youth group, Sunday school, missions to Haiti, a music ministry, and social circle. Members make prayer shawls for people that are ill, and they have a book group, potluck dinners, and a thrift shop. (Courtesy of the Amesbury Public Library.)

Five

Celebration and Remembrance

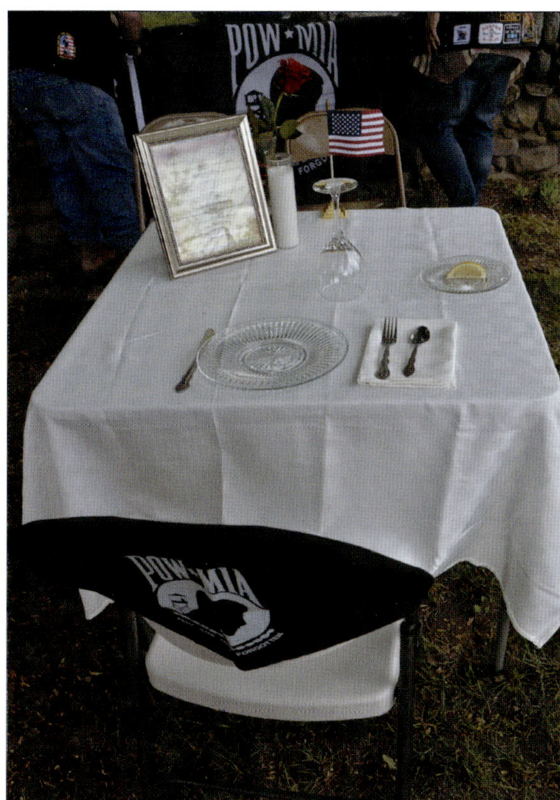

This empty chair represents all of the Americans that are among the missing in each of the military branches. Each item on the table symbolizes how family members keep the faith and hope that their son or daughter will one day come home. On Veterans Day and Memorial Day, the table and chair are set up by families to remind people that servicemen and women are missing or prisoners of war. (Photograph by the author.)

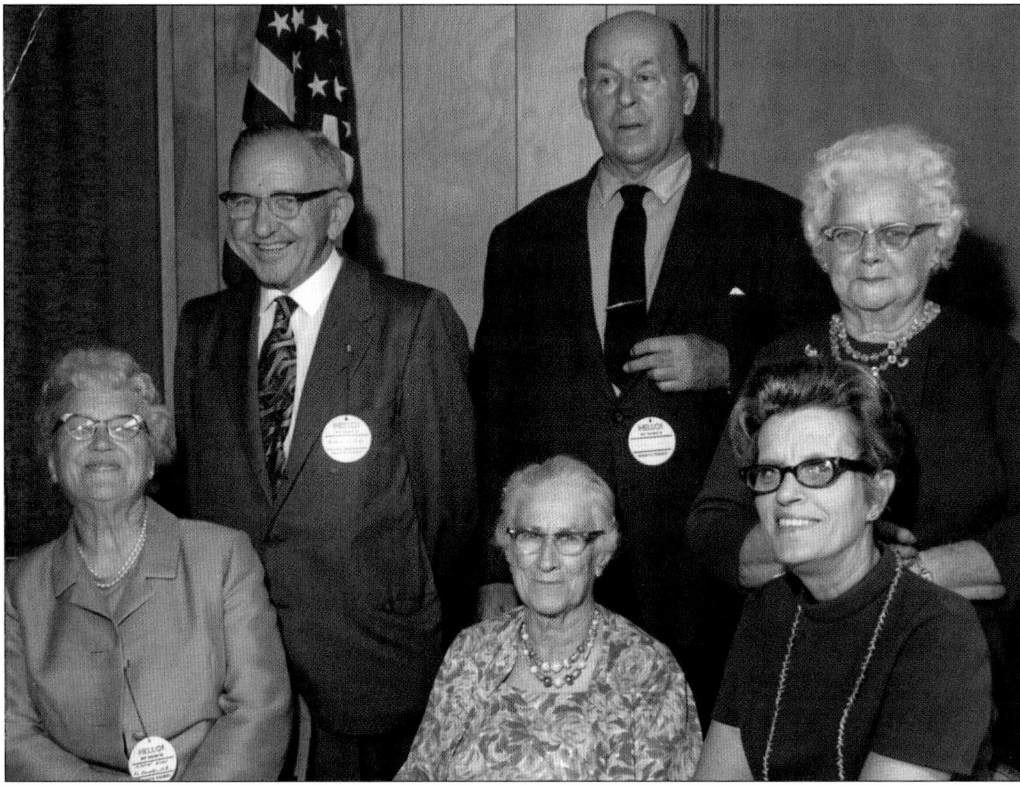

Anthony and Susannah Colby were some of the first settlers of Amesbury. Pictured here is a Colby family reunion from the 1960s. The family continues to have reunions yearly. In 2014, the reunion was held in Amesbury. There were people from all over the United States that came home. They were able to walk the same path that their ancestors did. (Both, courtesy of Kathy Colby.)

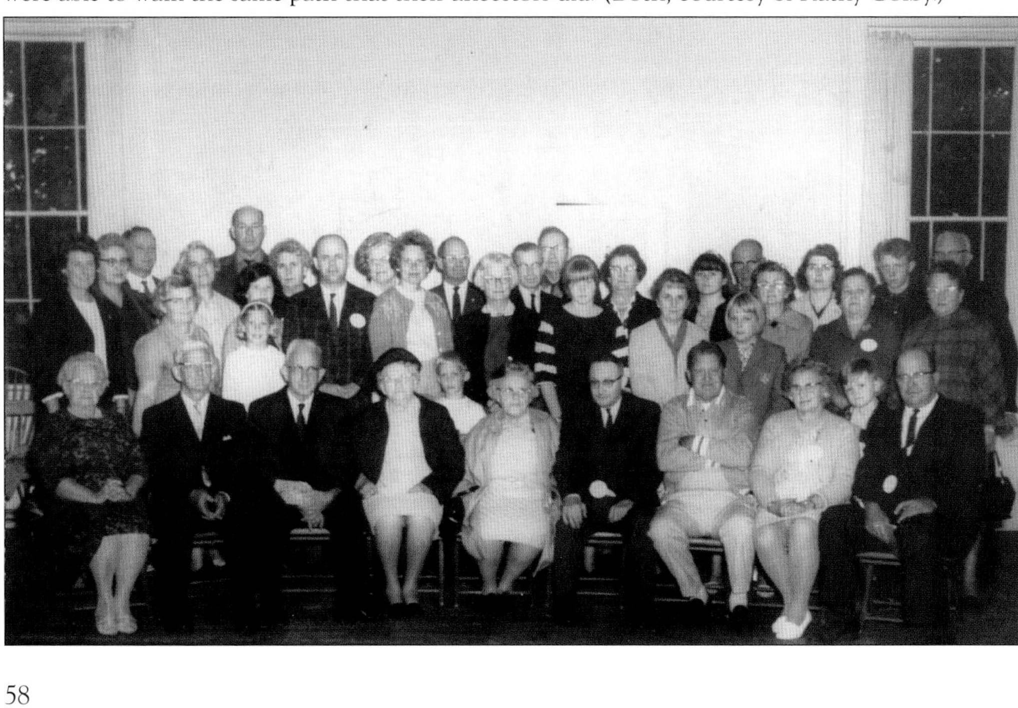

Chief Kevin Ouellet is a third-generation resident of Amesbury. He began his career with the Amesbury Police Department in 1980, when he joined the Amesbury Auxiliary Police. He graduated from the 12-week K-9 academy in 1981 and became a K-9 officer. In 1984, he was made a full-time officer. In 2013, Ouellet became chief of the police force. (Photograph by Joey Walker; courtesy of Chief Kevin Ouellet.)

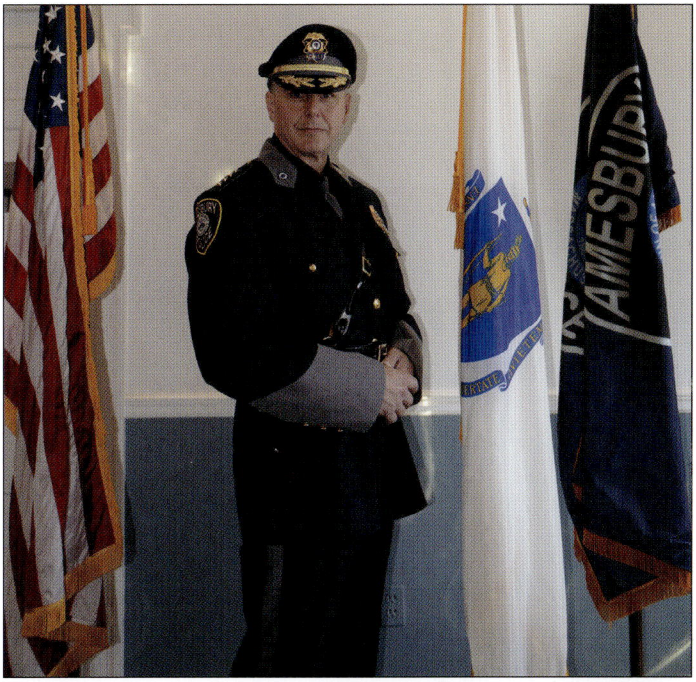

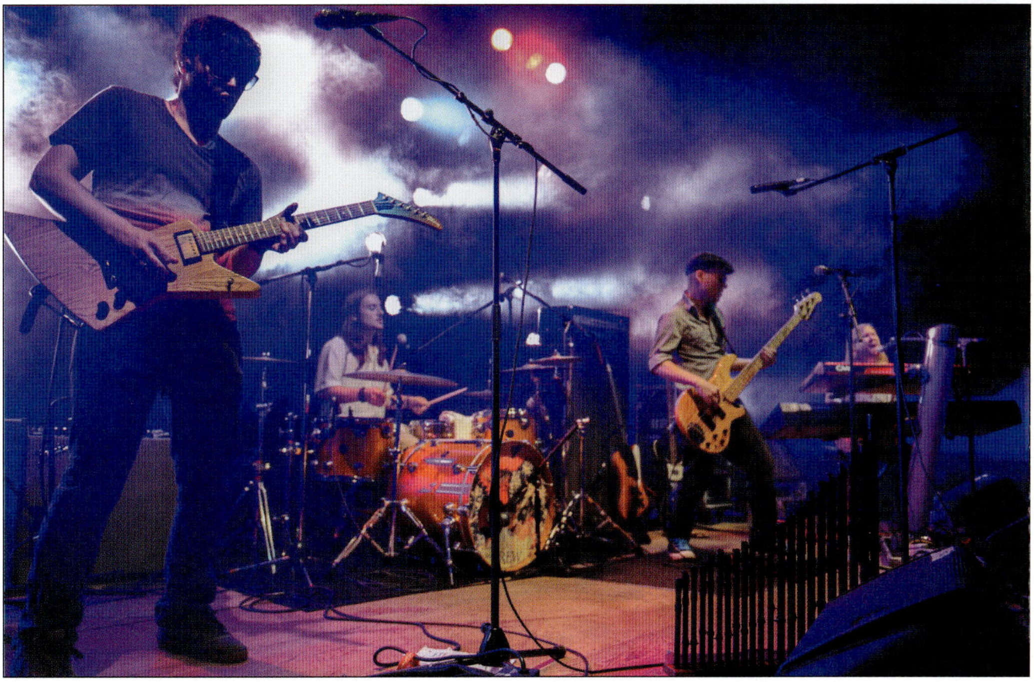

Chris Plante, Dave Drouin, Joe Plante, and Kelly Kane started a band in 2001 when they were students at Amesbury High School. The name of the band was Blue Fungus Blue. In 2002, they changed their name to the Brew. Once out of school, they took the band on the road and opened for renowned artists across the country. Aaron Zaroulis replaced Kane on drums, and the band played on. On August 24, 2013, the Brew had their last show at the Amesbury Sports Park. (Photograph by Joey Walker.)

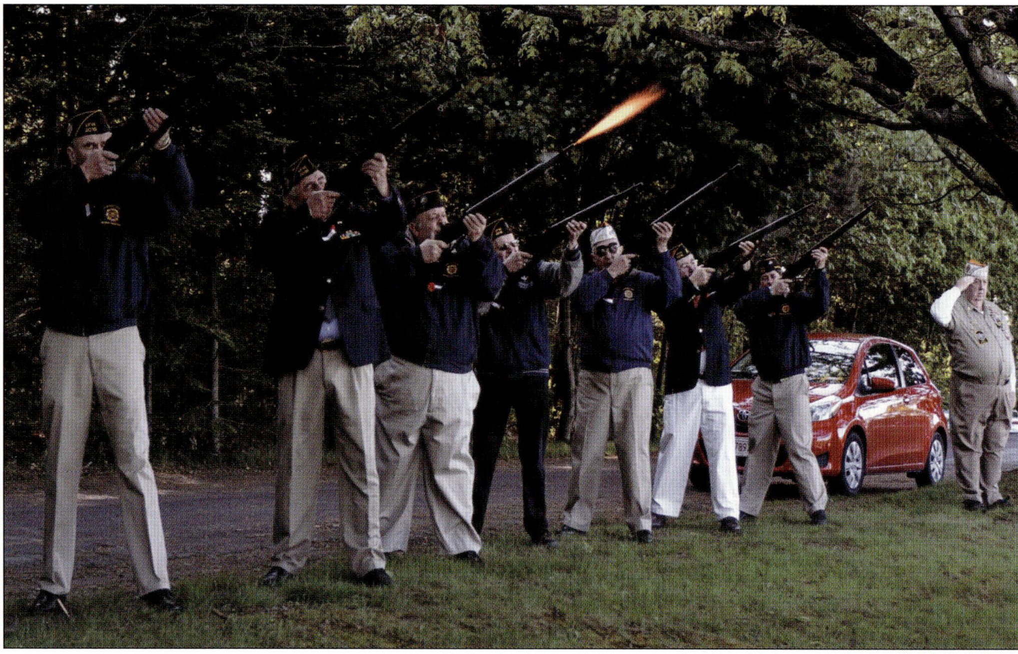

Pictured here during a Memorial Day remembrance are, from left to right, John White, Bob Smith, Mark Vedrani, Richard Bailey, Dick O'Donnell, John Carter, Charlie Bennett, and Jake Brohel saluting. The men and women of the Richard F. O'Brien VFW Post 2016 go to all of the cemeteries and memorials to remember all of the Amesbury veterans. This is an annual ceremony. (Photograph by Joey Walker.)

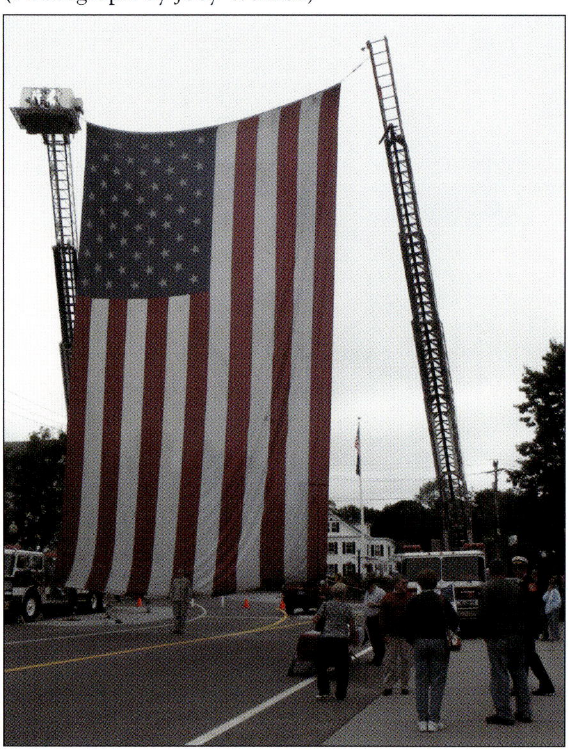

On June 25, 2011, Amesbury was honored to have the Patriotic Flag. The flag is a tribute to all of the first responders, second responders, military personnel, and all of the families and the family members that were lost on September 11, 2001. A big thank-you to Gary and Bonnie Crocker and Wayne Louth for bringing the flag to Amesbury. (Photograph by the author.)

Frances Justin was in school when the doughboy statue was first dedicated in 1929. On May 18, 2014, she was honored at the rededication of the doughboy by unveiling the statue to the crowd that came out for the ceremony. (Photograph by Joey Walker.)

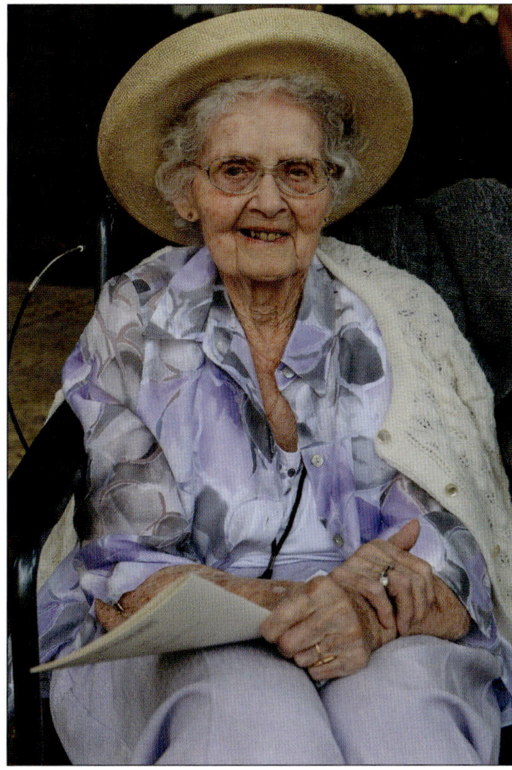

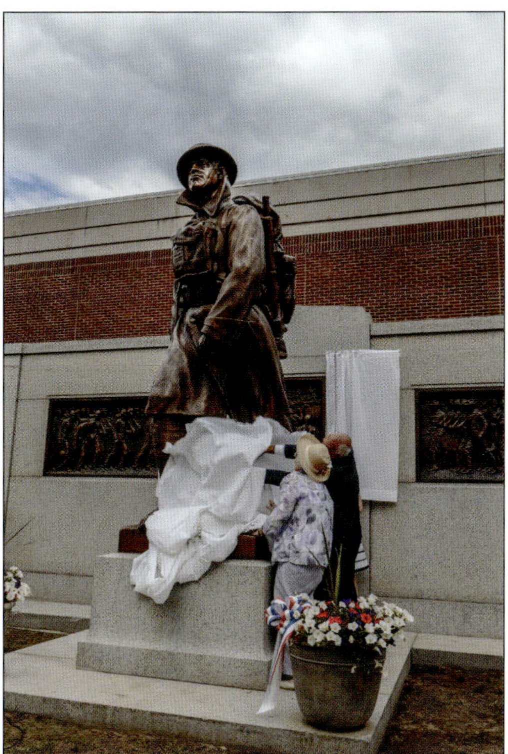

The doughboy statue was first dedicated on November 11, 1929, and it was changing color due to the weather it had endured for so many years. Volunteers started fundraising to bring the doughboy back to its original condition. The rededication was held on Sunday, May 18, 2014. (Photograph by Joey Walker.)

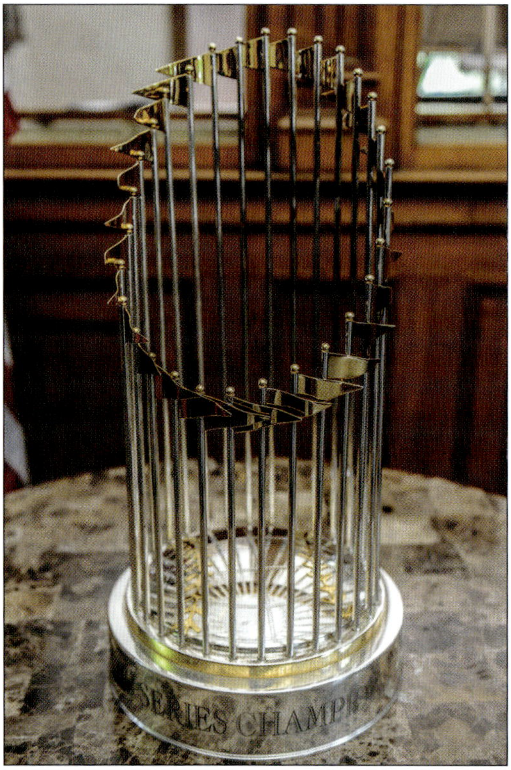

The year 2013 belonged to the Red Sox, as they won the World Series. The trophy was on tour around different cities in Massachusetts, and Amesbury was one of the stops. (Photograph by Joey Walker.)

The Amesbury Public Library opened its doors in 1902. The institution celebrated its 100th anniversary in 2002. The library provides resources for educational, cultural, and personal development and social and recreational needs. The library is the center of the community. (Photograph by the author.)

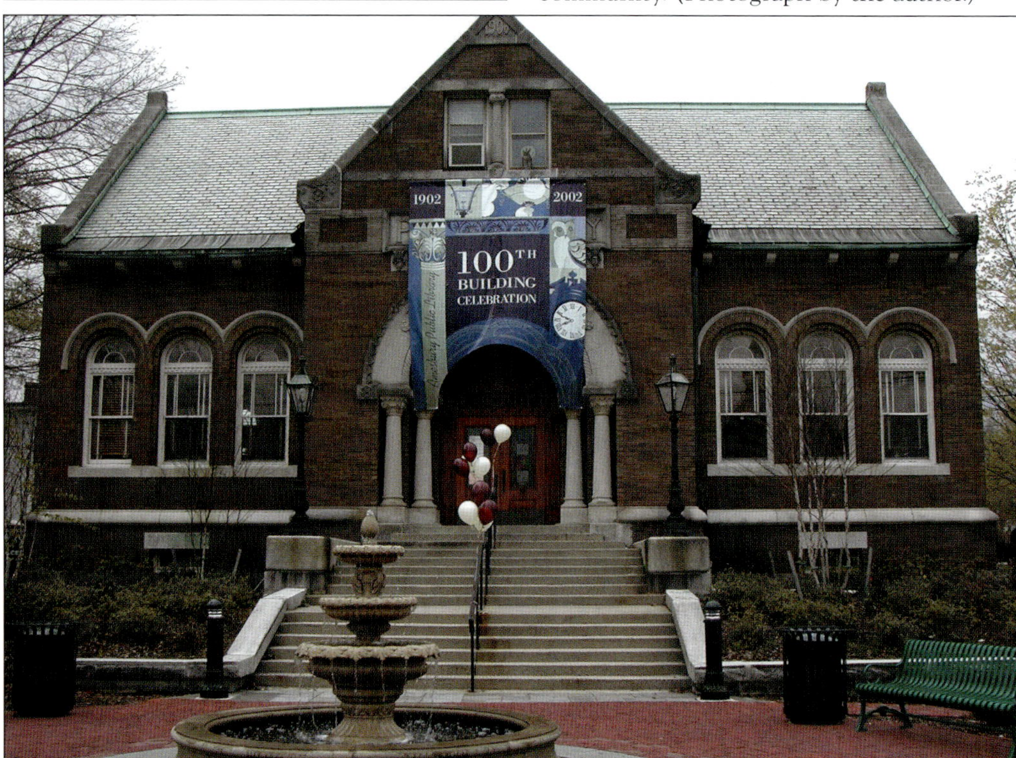

This statue of Josiah Bartlett looks on as the militia is gathering to march to Alliance Park. April 1975 was the start of a yearlong celebration of the United States' bicentennial. At 1:00 p.m., the church bells rang throughout Amesbury, calling men to arms. (Courtesy of the Amesbury Public Library.)

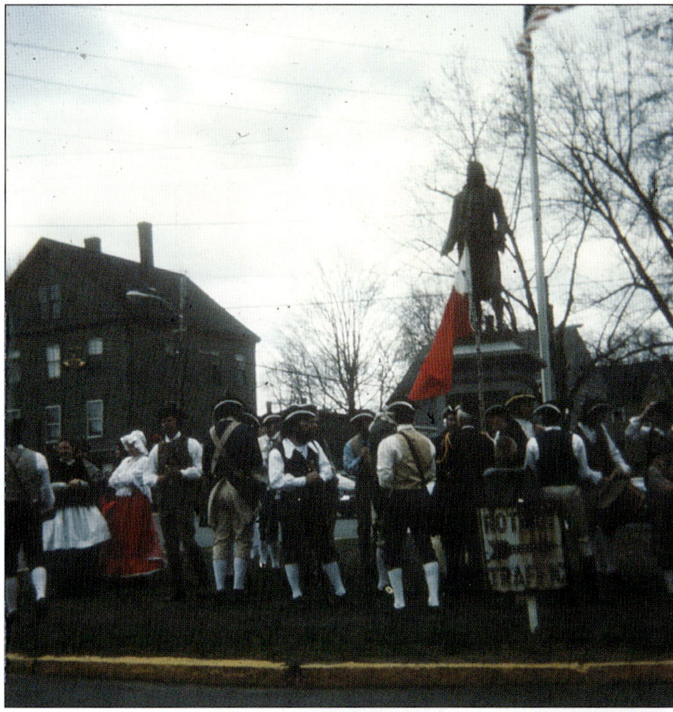

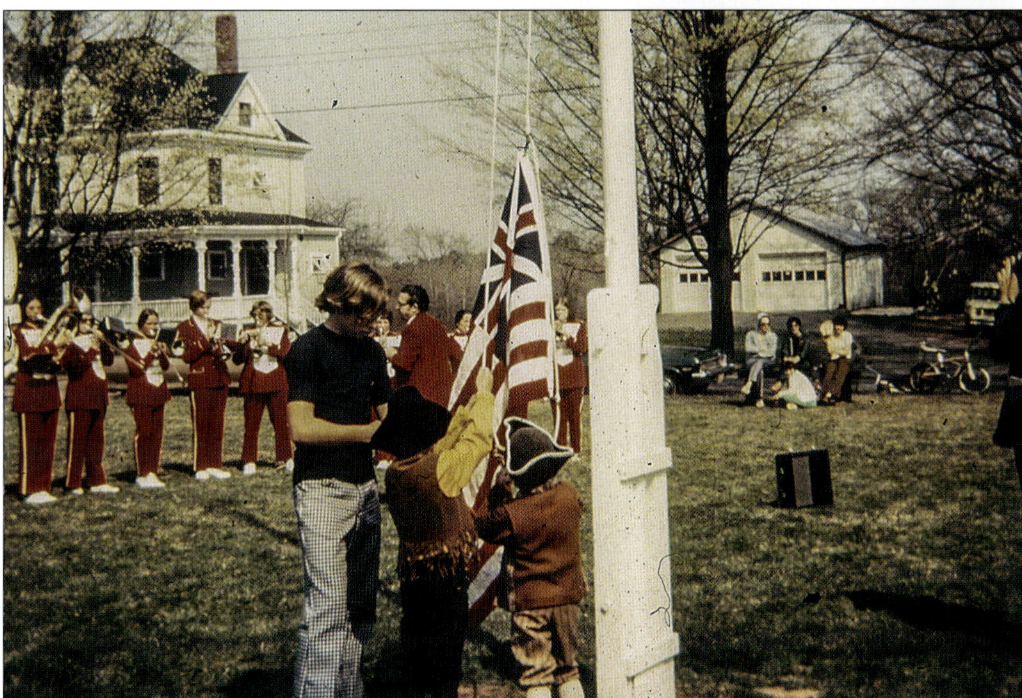

Pictured here is the flag-raising at the dedication ceremony at the Monroe Street training field in April 1976. The theme, "Spirit of 76," was announced, and there were speeches about the historical significance of the training field where Gen. George Washington reviewed troops. (Courtesy of the Amesbury Public Library.)

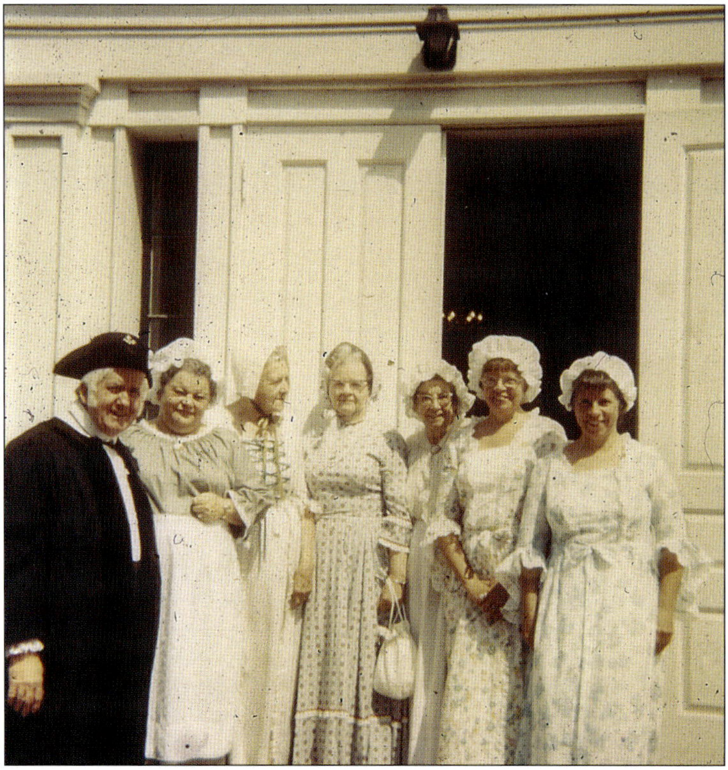

The community is celebrating the bicentennial in July 1976. Pictured here in Colonial dress are, from left to right, Earl Young, Charlotte Young, Esther Burke, Irene Wilson, Frances Brown, and Betty and Ernestine Goodwin. (Courtesy of the Amesbury Public Library.)

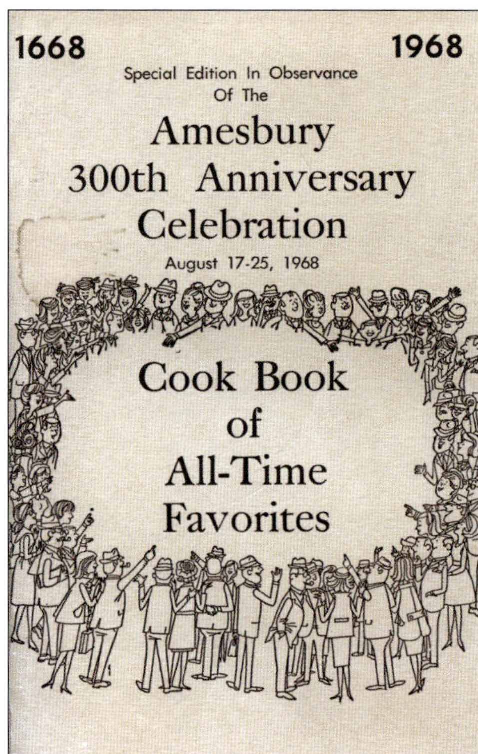

The *Amesbury Cookbook* was produced for the 300th anniversary of the city of Amesbury. Many of the recipes in the book have come down from generation to generation. A list of herbs that the earlier settlers used is included. (Photograph by the author.)

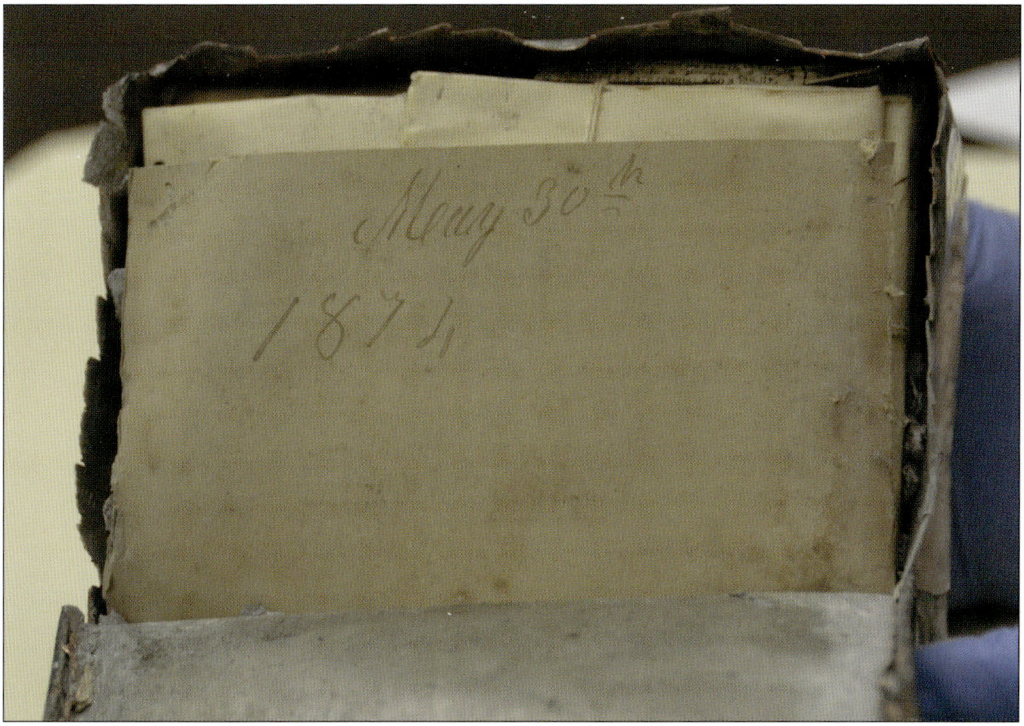

On May 30, 1874, a time capsule was placed inside the Civil War monument in Union Cemetery. Paul Janciewicz and Dennis "Ski" Iworsky, cochairs of the Amesbury Veterans Memorial Restoration Committee, armed with a metal detector, were able to find the capsule. On June 15, 2015, the time capsule was opened. Inside were coins, a 3¢ stamp on an envelope addressed to John Currier, 1874 newspapers, lists of names of members of the Warren's Lodge, and a list of names of soldiers from Amesbury and Salisbury that served in the Civil War. Janciewicz is looking at the list of Amesbury soldiers that fought in the Civil War. History was clearly made on this day. It was an honor to be able to witness this event in which brave men that served were remembered. (Photograph by the author.)

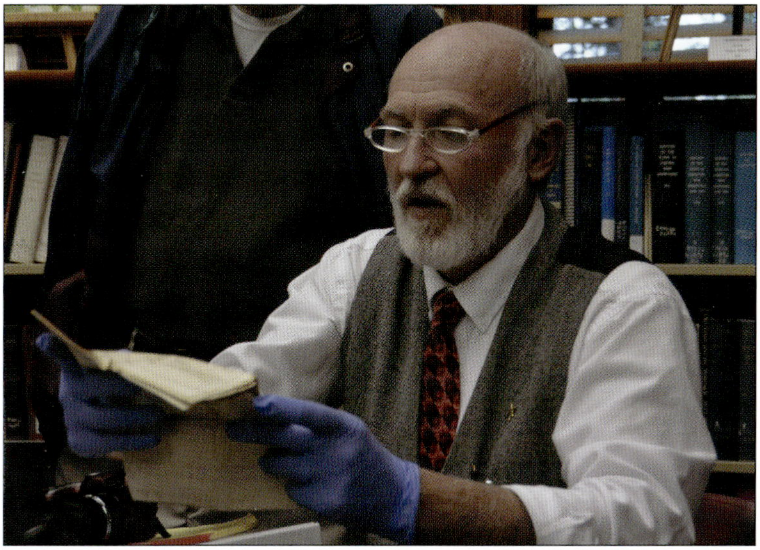

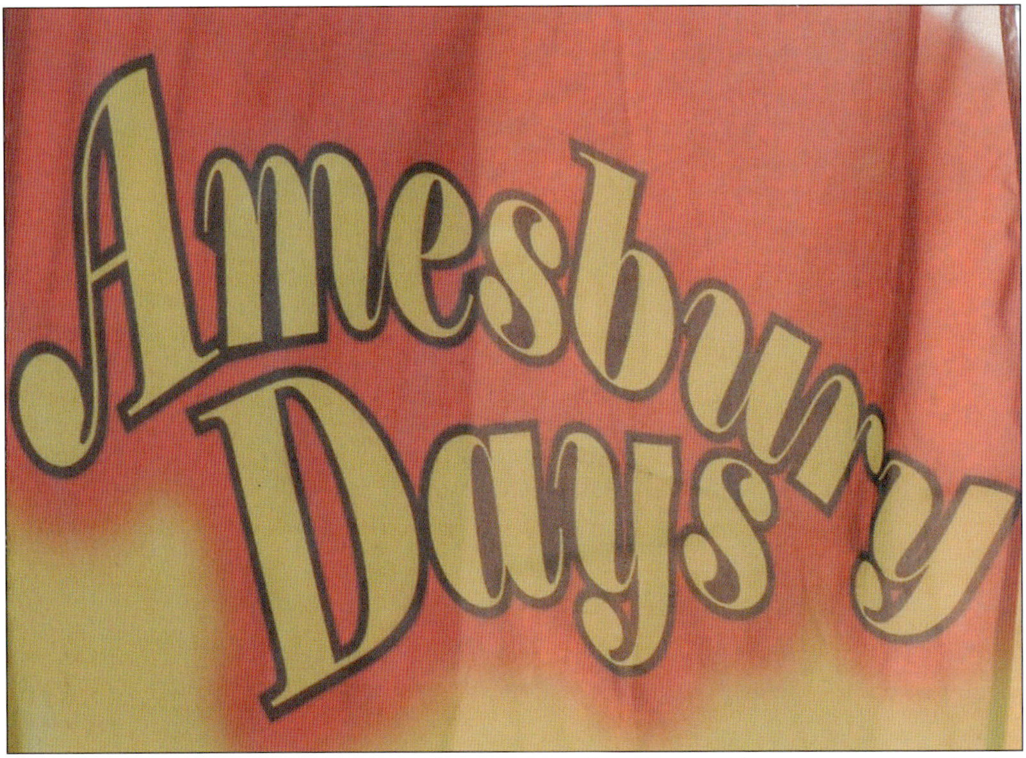

Amesbury Days began as a one-day celebration for mill workers and businesses and was held at Lake Gardner. Now, 116 years later, the city is still celebrating Amesbury Days. It runs about 10 days from late June through the Fourth of July. Entertainment is centered in the millyard. Pictured below are, from left to right, Dottie Therrien, Janet (Trahan) Brunell, Maryann Brannan, and Grace Trahan doing the chicken dance. The festivities include a brew festival, car show, senior citizen cookout, block party, and farmers' market. (Both, photograph by the author.)

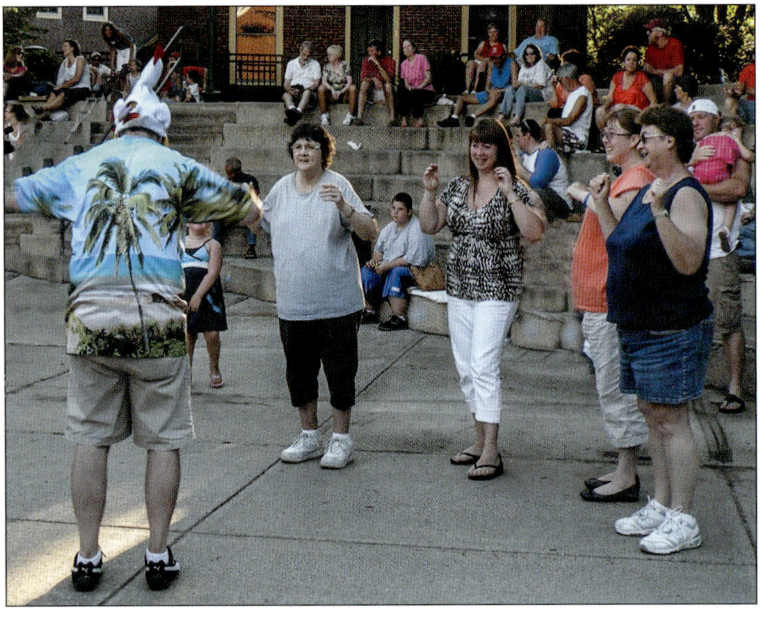

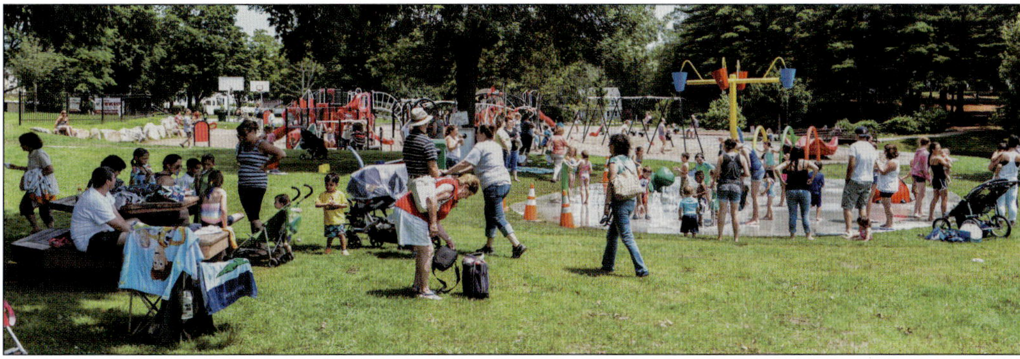

Kid's day in the park is part of the Amesbury Day celebration sponsored by the Amesbury Youth Service Department. Kids are reveling in the new sprinklers, enjoying the park. One of the annual events is the teddy bear parade. (Photograph by Joey Walker.)

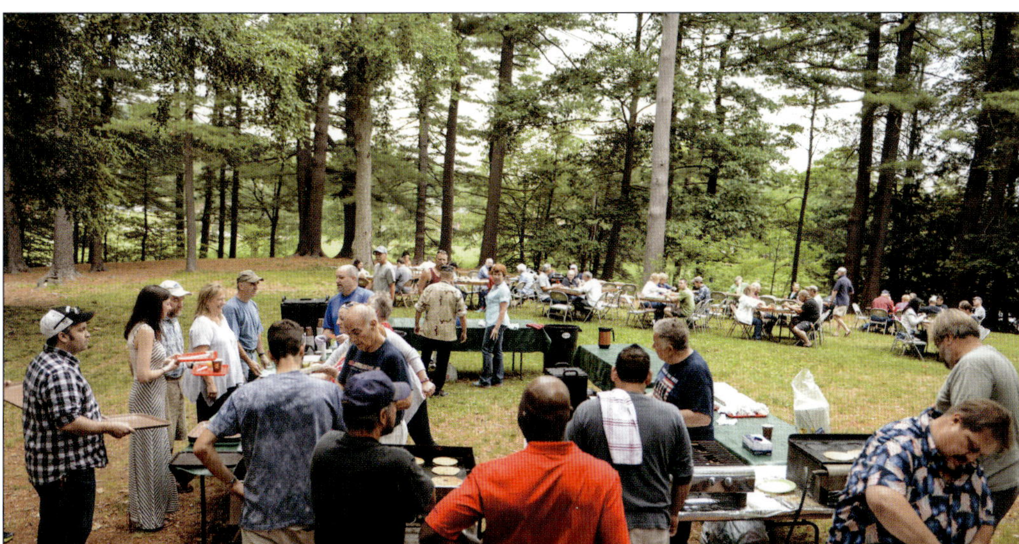

Pancakes in the Pines is sponsored by Amesbury Rock Church. Pancakes are cooked up on the grill at this annual event in July. Residents come out and enjoy their breakfast amongst the tall pine trees. (Photograph by Joey Walker.)

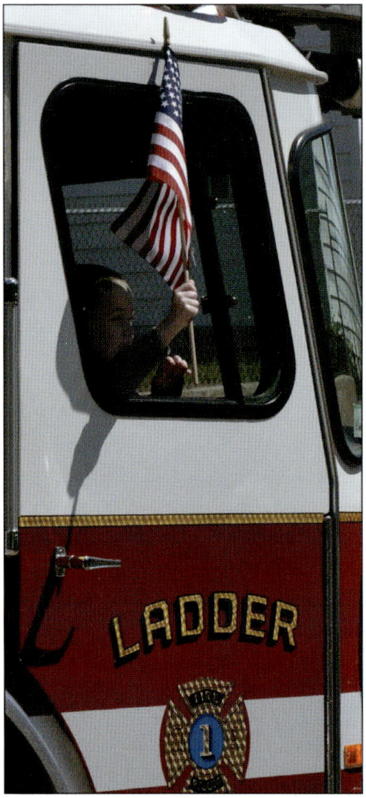

Connor Calderwood, son of fireman Todd Calderwood, rides proudly in the Amesbury fire truck in the Memorial Day parade in 2013. Every year, all of the veterans, past and present, are honored with a parade and a ceremony, which takes place at Landry Stadium. (Photograph by Joey Walker.)

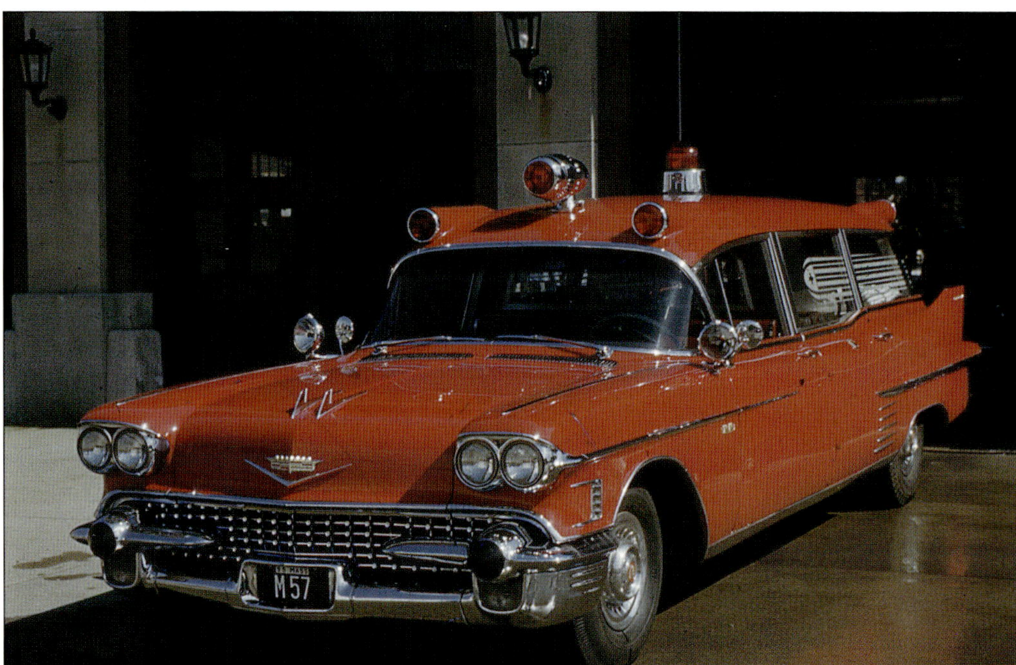

Amesbury Fire Department has a new 1957 Cadillac ambulance. This ambulance had all of the bells and whistles that the department needed. (Courtesy of the Amesbury Public Library)

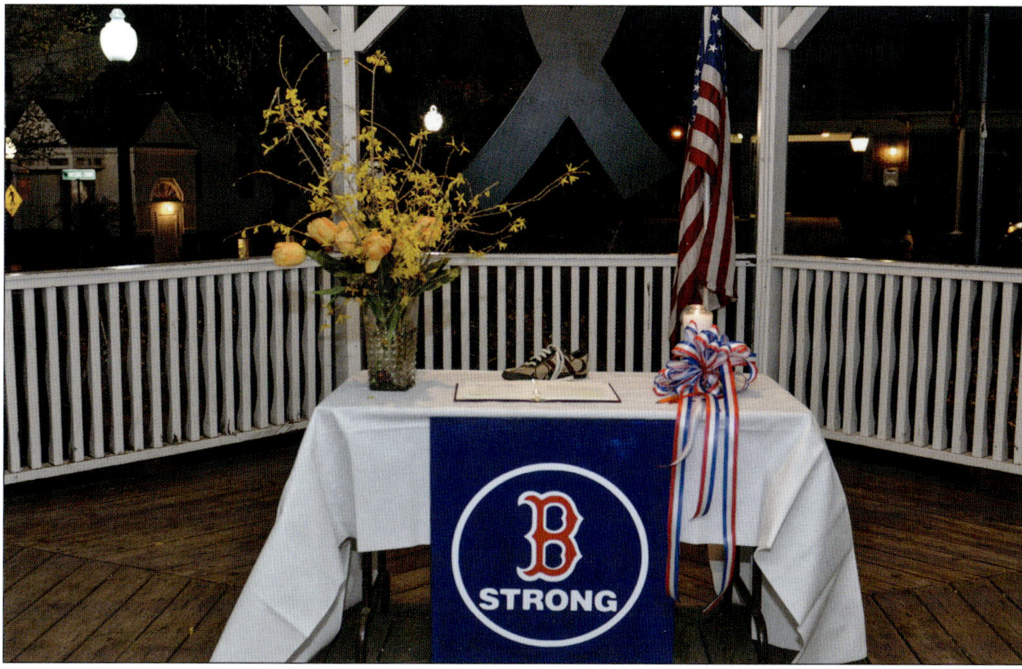

On April 15, 2013, a bomb was placed along the Boston Marathon route in Boston. The Amesbury community came together for a vigil for the people that were involved in this devastating occurrence. (Photograph by the author.)

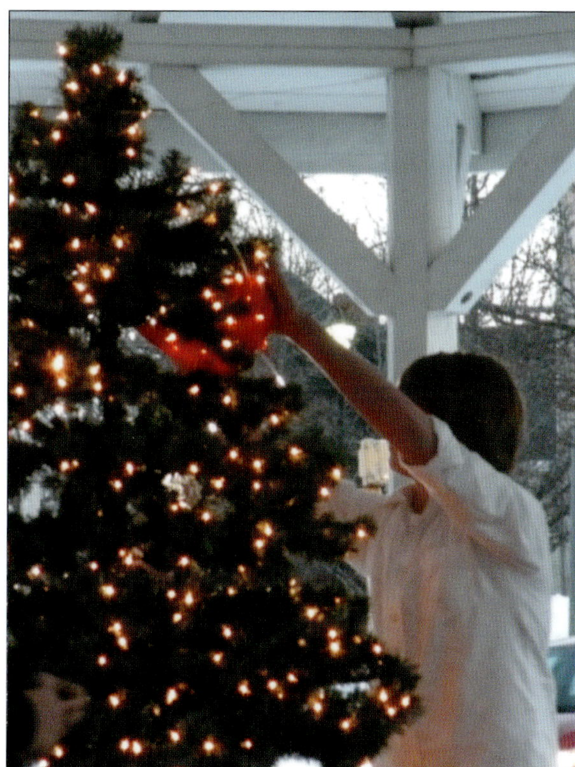

On December 14, 2012, a tragedy occurred at Sandy Hook Elementary School in Newtown, Connecticut. The students at Amesbury Middle School made valentines to be sent to the Sandy Hook community. City officials and students were present to add hearts to a tree during a day of remembrance. (Photograph by the author.)

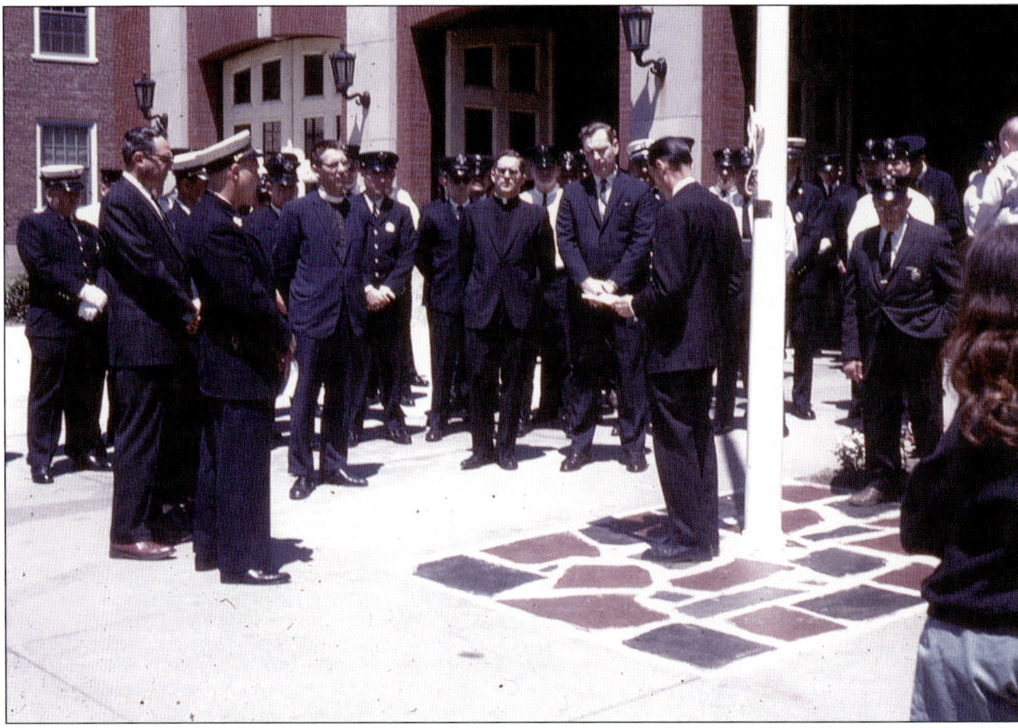

The flagpole in the front of the Amesbury Fire Department was dedicated in the memory of Chief James E. Feltham. Chief Feltham was a member of the Amesbury Fire Department from May 2, 1902, until July 1, 1939. (Courtesy of the Amesbury Public Library.)

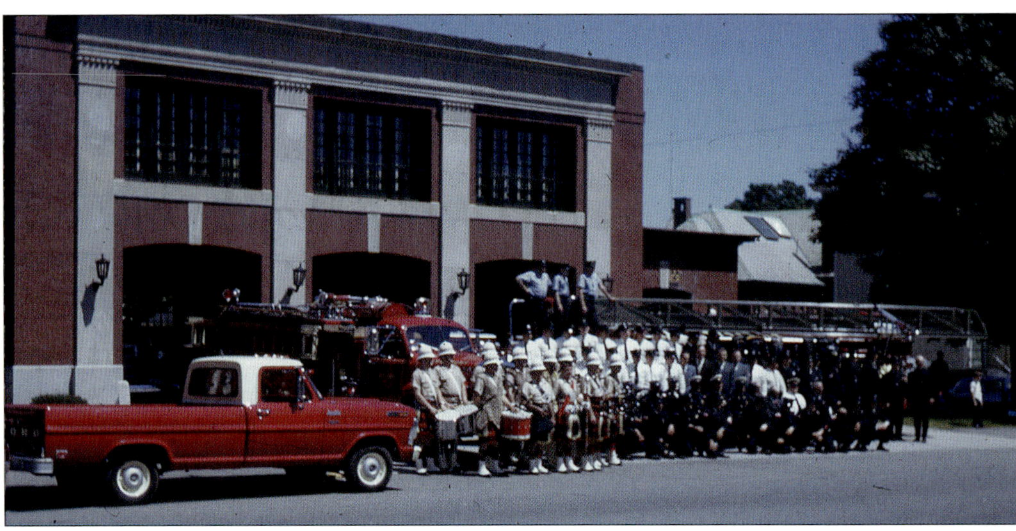

Members of the Amesbury Fire Department are lined up for the parade to the firemen's memorial in Union Cemetery. This parade was in conjunction with the 300th anniversary of Amesbury. The Clan Wallace is also pictured here, a pipe band from Beverly, Massachusetts. (Courtesy of the Amesbury Public Library.)

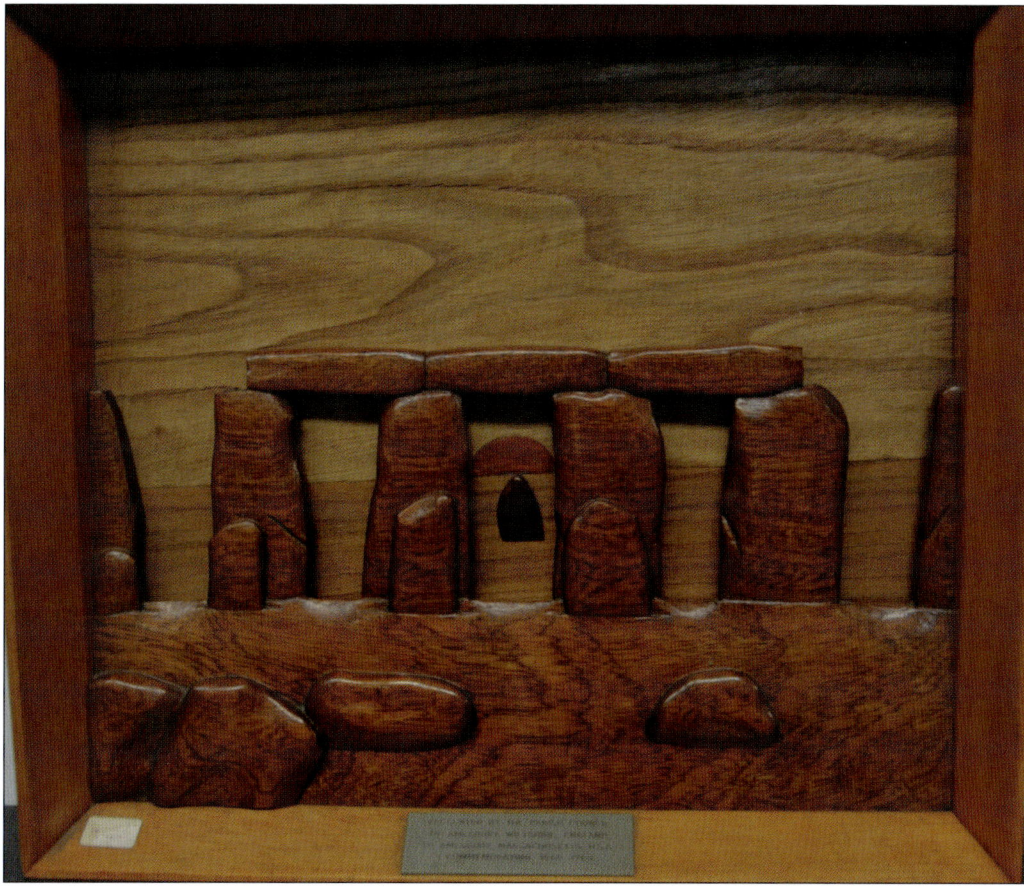

Amesbury celebrated the 300th anniversary of the town in 1968. Councilor Austin Underwood came from Amesbury, England, to present the town with gifts. One of the gifts was a hand-carved wooden Stonehenge. Underwood also presented a short pictorial history of Amesbury, England, and a map of that town. (Photograph by the author; courtesy of the Amesbury Public Library.)

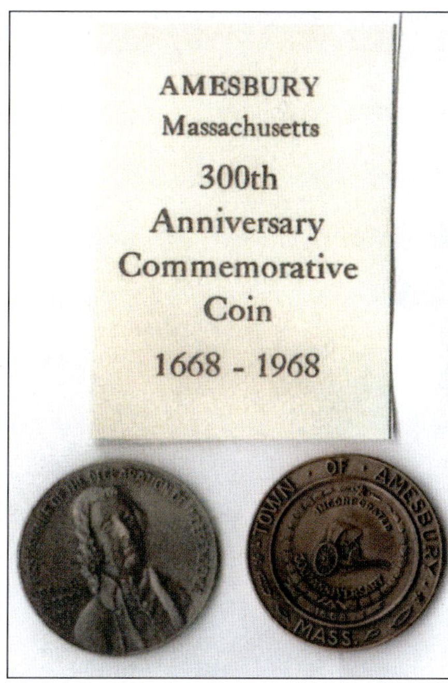

As part of the 300th anniversary of Amesbury, commemorative coins were created with Josiah Bartlett, signer of the Declaration of Independence, on the front and the town of Amesbury with the incorporation date on the back. The coins were sold as part of the celebration. (Photograph by the author.)

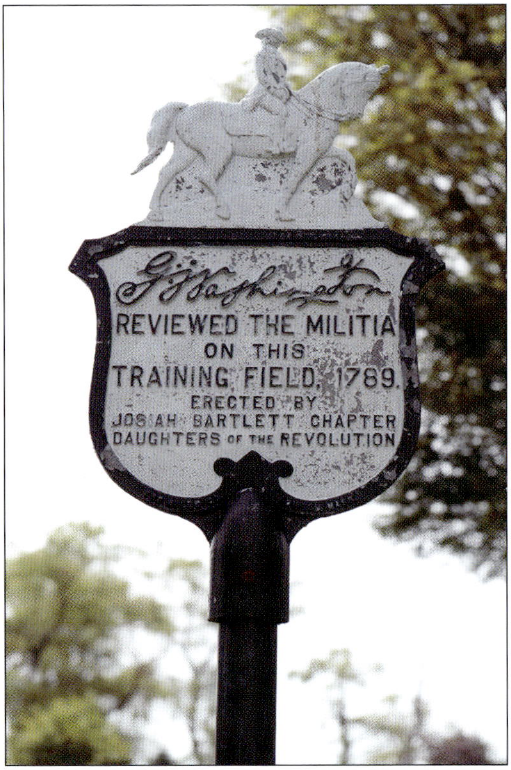

In 1725, Salisbury, Massachusetts, voters voted to have a training field. The training field was part of Salisbury until it was annexed to Amesbury in 1886. The training field on the corner of Monroe and Portsmouth Streets is where George Washington spoke to his troops in 1789. The training field is one of the Amesbury treasures. The Amesbury Improvement Association takes care of the grounds. (Photograph by Joey Walker.)

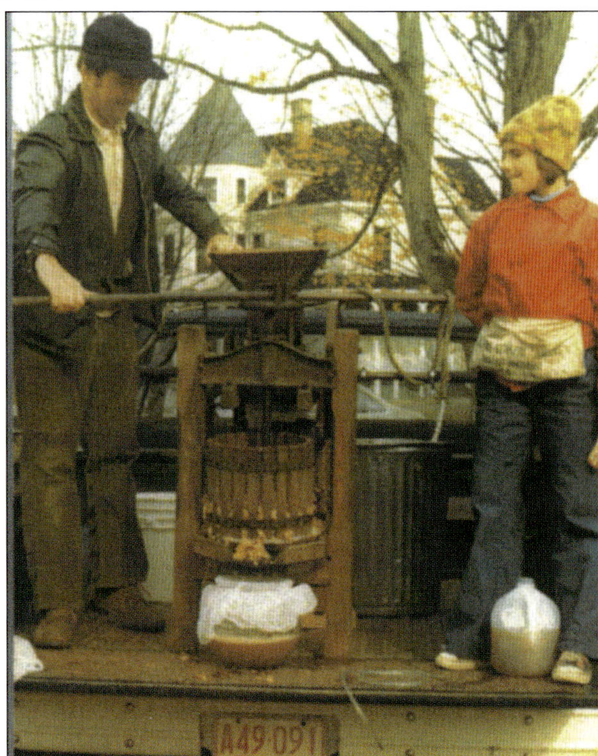

The second annual Training Field Day was held on September 21, 1975, to mark the anniversary of Gen. George Washington's stop in Amesbury during the Revolutionary War. Ronald Gagnon and his son Michael are cranking up the cider press to celebrate the event. (Courtesy of the Amesbury Public Library.)

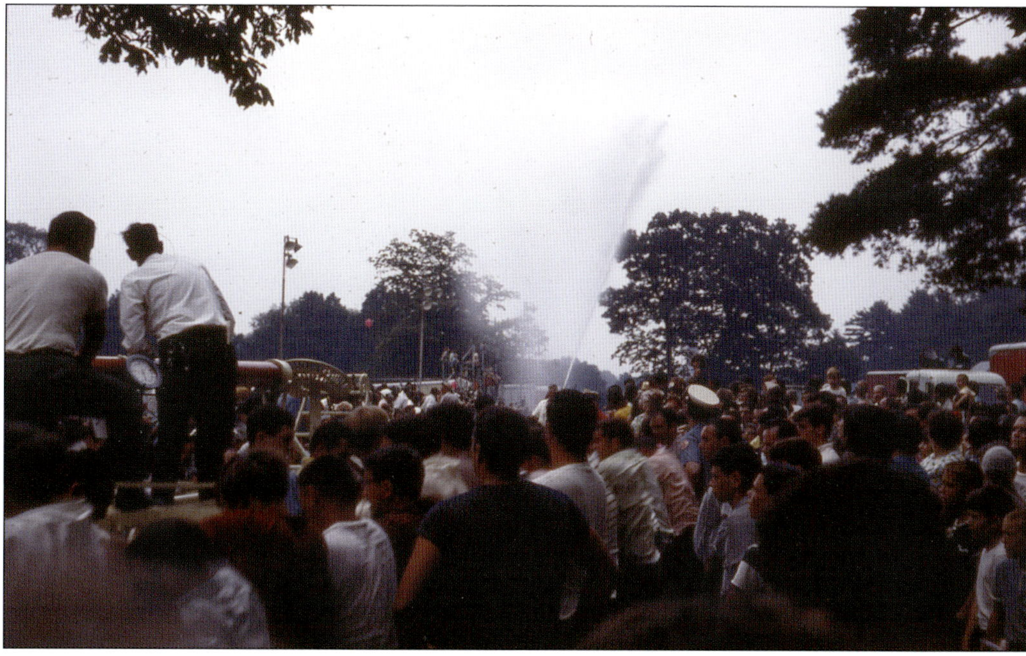

As part of Amesbury Days, the firefighters' union sponsored the first full-scale muster. Joining the Powow No. 1 were hand tubs from New England. This event was the first muster of the season, with hundreds of spectators present for the event. (Courtesy of the Amesbury Public Library.)

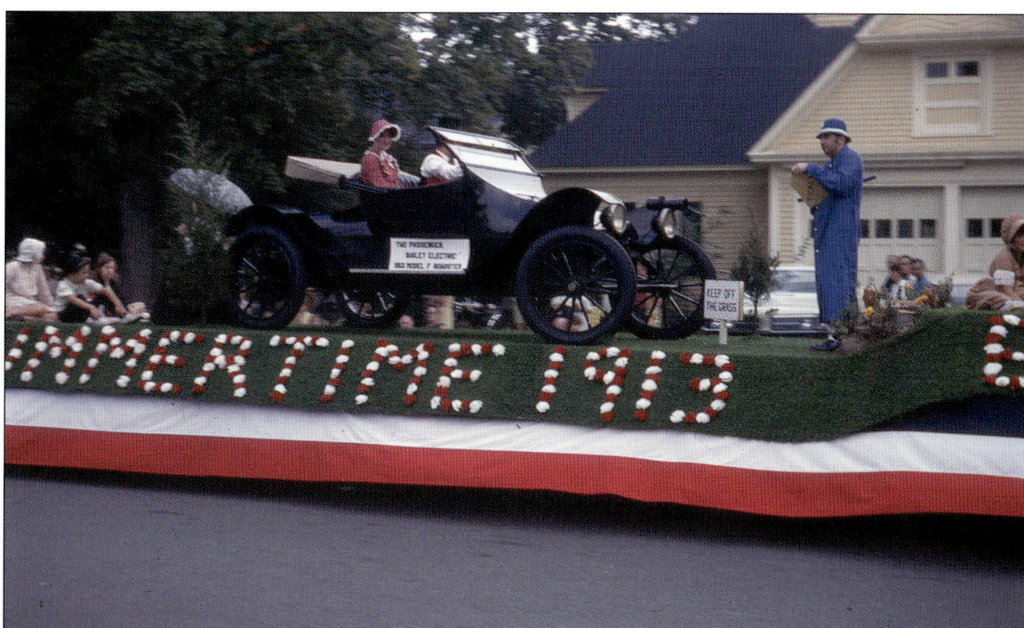

This float captures the spirit of the summer of 1913 with a Bailey Electric two-passenger car. It looks like the police officer is writing out a ticket for them because they are parking on the grass. (Courtesy of the Amesbury Public Library.)

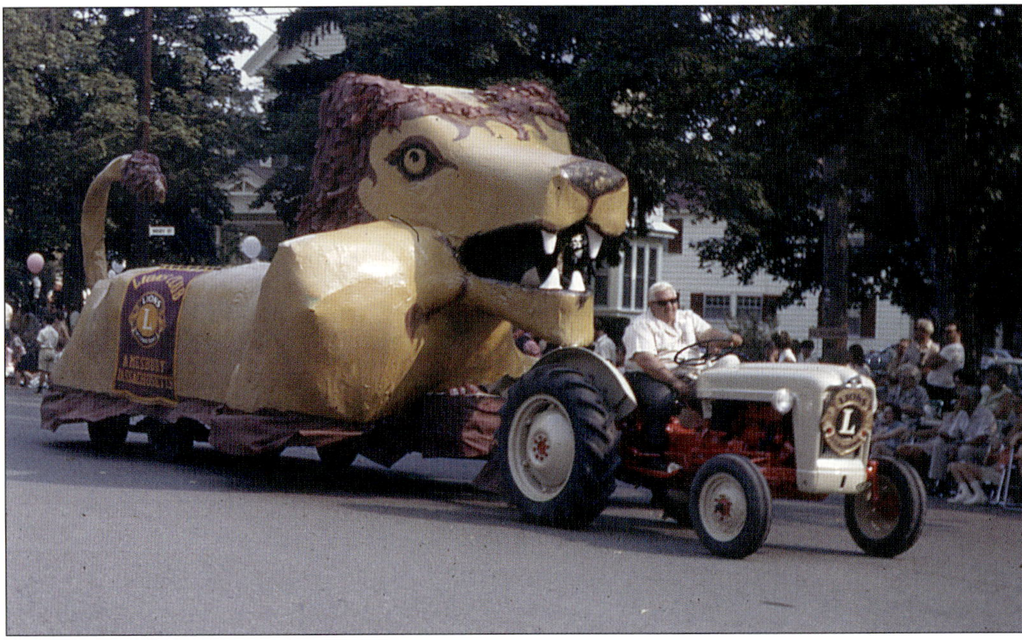

This float was built in 1983 by the Amesbury Lions and their families. They were helped with the design by a set designer from the Amesbury Playhouse. R.G. Watkins Company donated space to build the float at its South Hampton Quonset huts. After mixing bucket after bucket of flour and water with newspaper, the papier-mâché lion was finished. It was towed to Norm Hamel's body shop on Monroe Street, where it was painted. (Courtesy of Steve Deorocki, Bob Pare, and the Amesbury Public Library.)

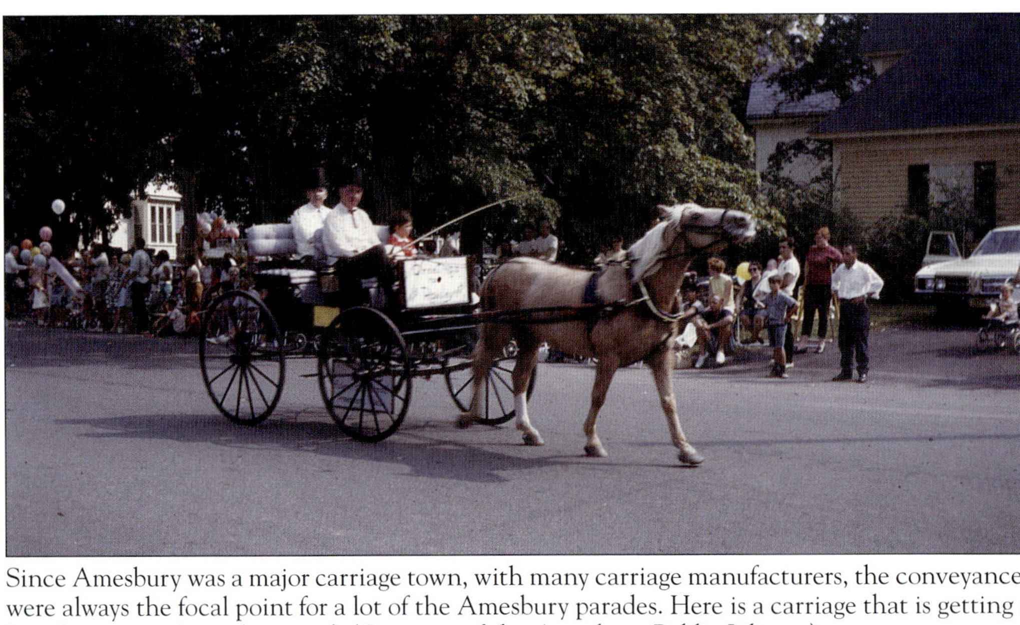

Since Amesbury was a major carriage town, with many carriage manufacturers, the conveyances were always the focal point for a lot of the Amesbury parades. Here is a carriage that is getting a lot of attention from the crowd. (Courtesy of the Amesbury Public Library.)

Six

Around Carriagetown

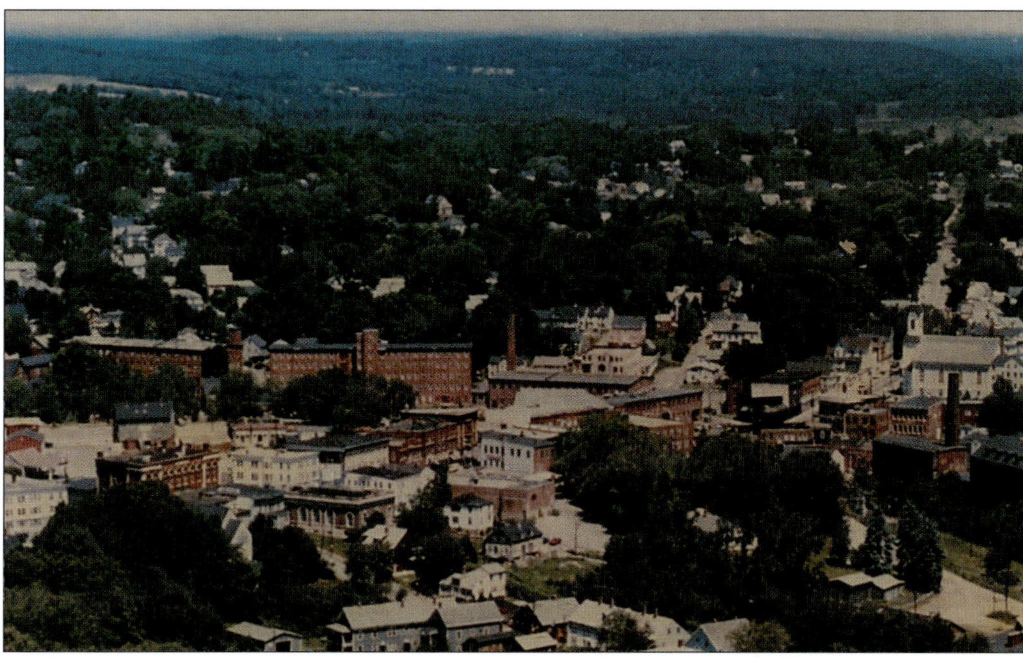

This is the Horton and Aubin Streets area of Amesbury, right off Main Street. A lot of the carriage workers lived in boardinghouses in this area. Mill buildings are visible as well as the old post office and the lower millyard. Off in the distance one can see New Hampshire. (Courtesy of the Amesbury Public Library.)

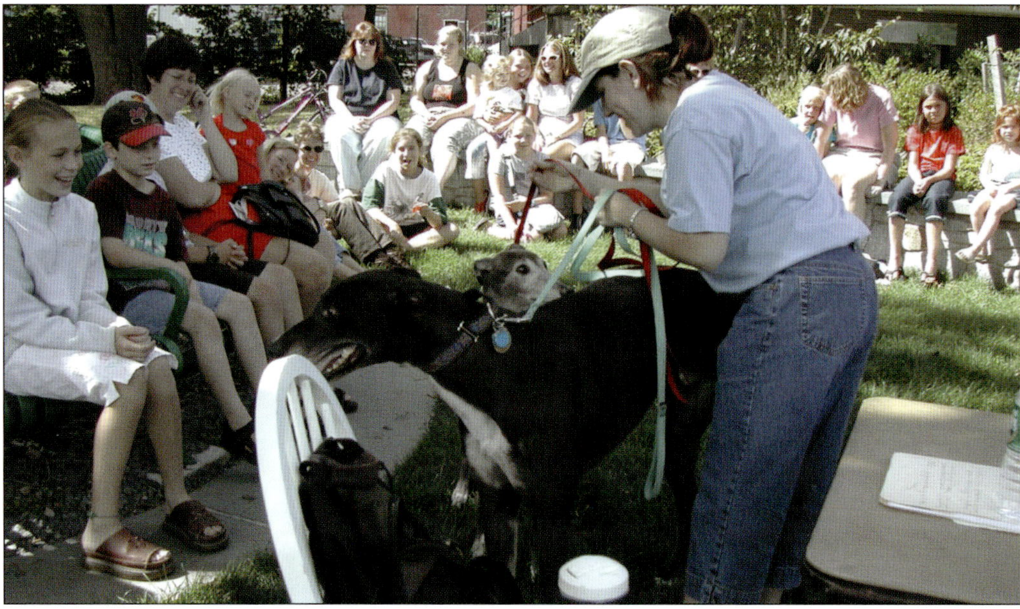

Greyhound Friends of Hopkinton, Massachusetts, came to Amesbury's Huntington Square to bring awareness to former racetrack greyhounds that are up for adoption. The audience was able to interact with the dogs and learn about grooming them, what type of temperament they have, and how they are around kids. (Photograph by the author.)

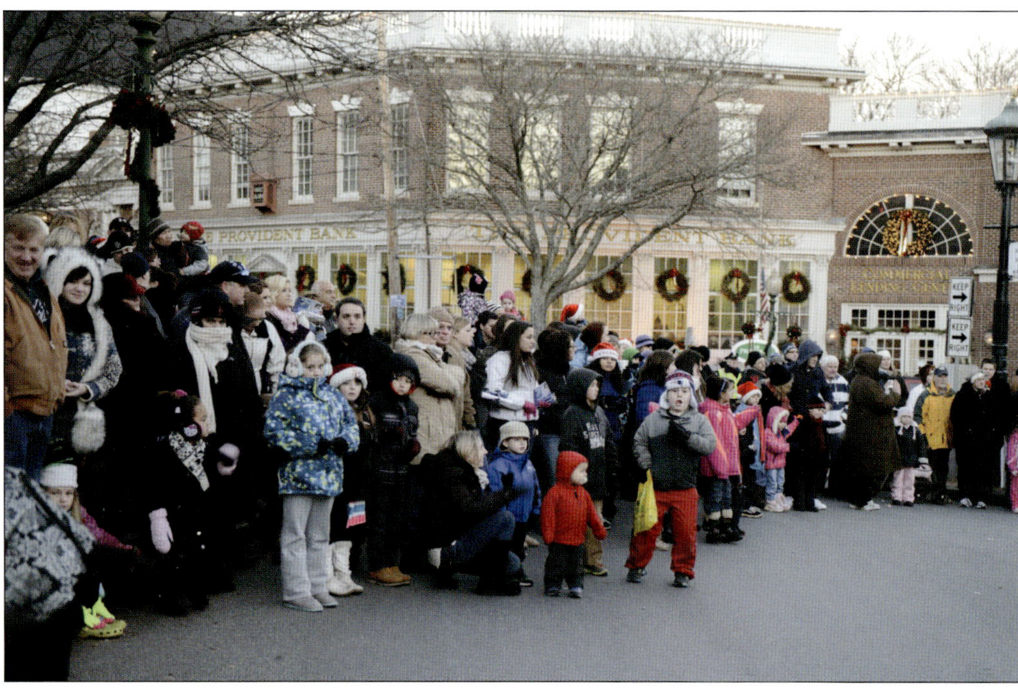

The Santa Claus parade is one of the highlights of the season. Children are lining up in Market Square anxiously waiting for the man himself to make an appearance. (Photograph by Joey Walker.)

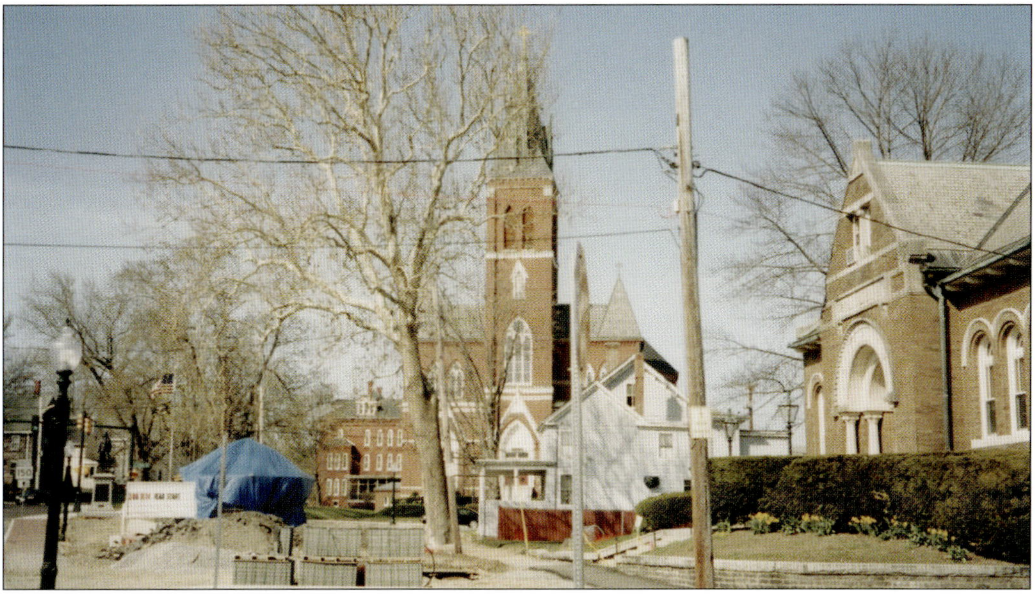

The addition of a gazebo was part of the redevelopment of the downtown area. In 2001, the city started construction, and today the gazebo is used for concerts, memorial programs, library programs, city events, and weddings. (Above, photograph by Dianne Cole; below, photograph by Joey Walker.)

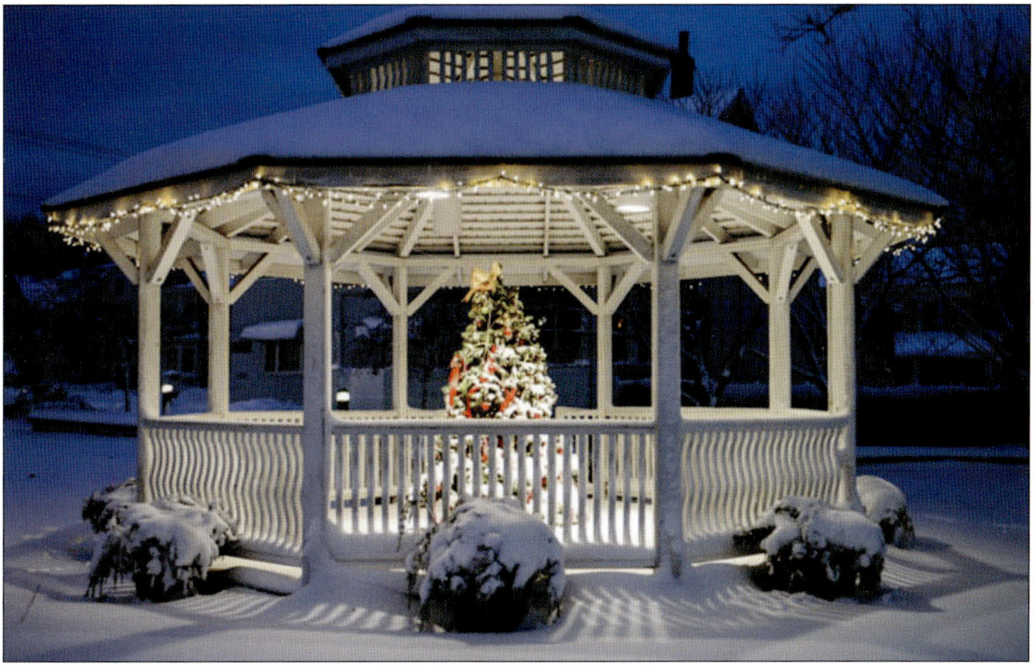

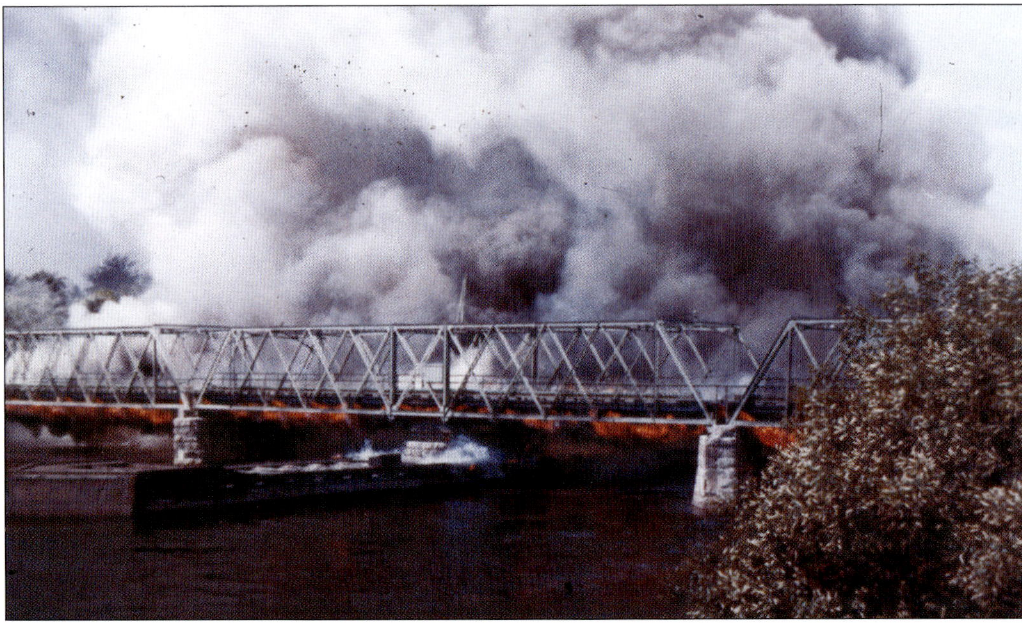

The Essex Merrimac Bridge connecting Amesbury and Deer Island was built in 1882 and destroyed by fire in 1964. (Courtesy of the Amesbury Public Library.)

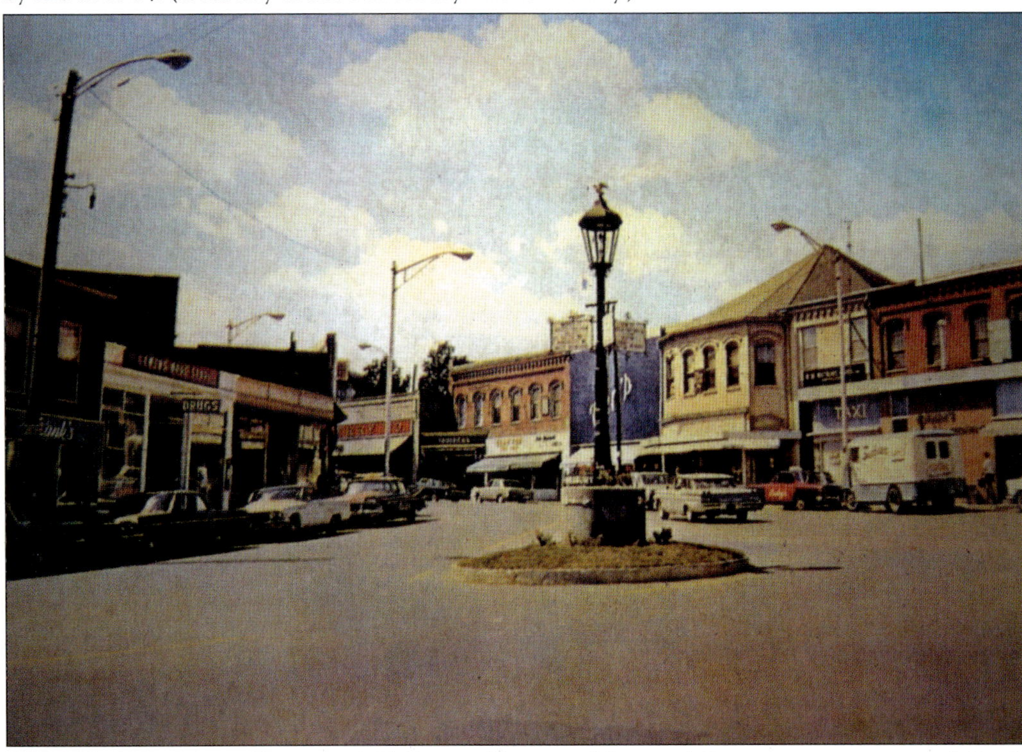

This is downtown Amesbury in 1965. Pictured here are Norman's Restaurant, a taxi stand, Ben's, and Newberry's on the right and a drugstore on the left. The only business that is still open is Ben's. They sell uniforms for police, firefighters, and construction workers. (Courtesy of the Amesbury Public Library.)

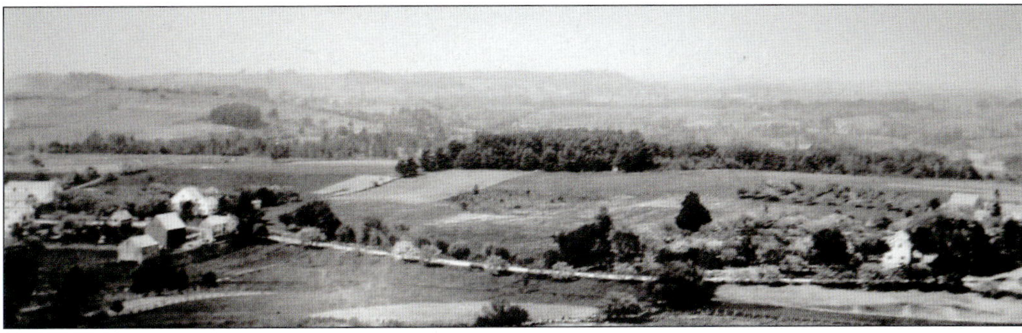

Powow Hill is the highest point in Amesbury, and at the top of the hill is Batchelder Park. It is the 11th-highest hill in Essex County. One can see the Atlantic Ocean from the top. There is a trail that leads to Lake Gardner. In the above photograph one can see how sparse the area was with homes. In the photograph below, there are houses on the side of the hill. (Above, courtesy of the Amesbury Public Library; below, photograph by the author.)

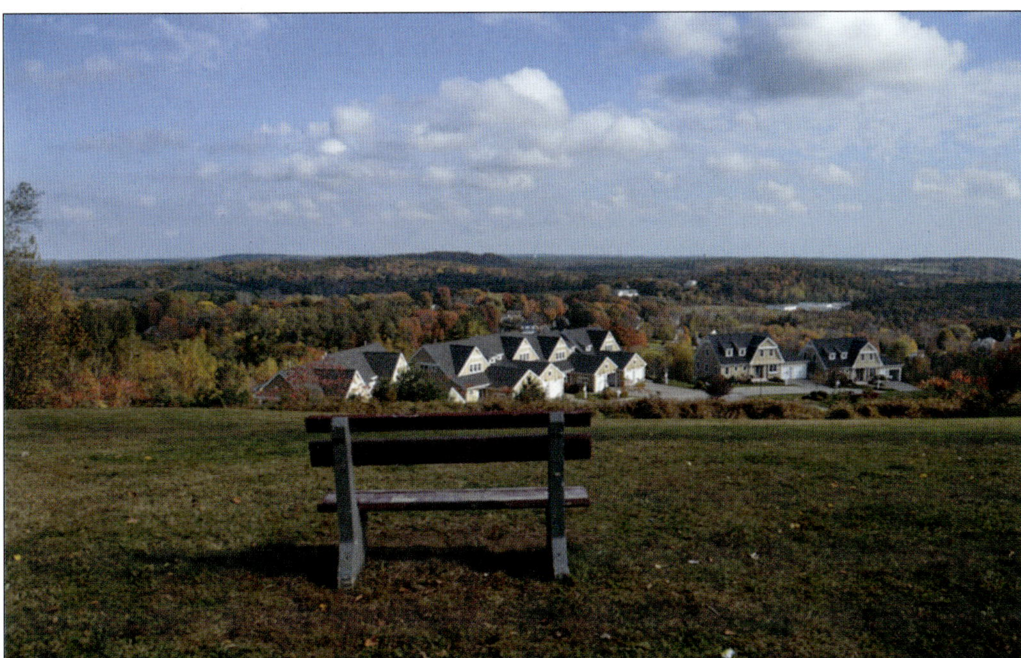

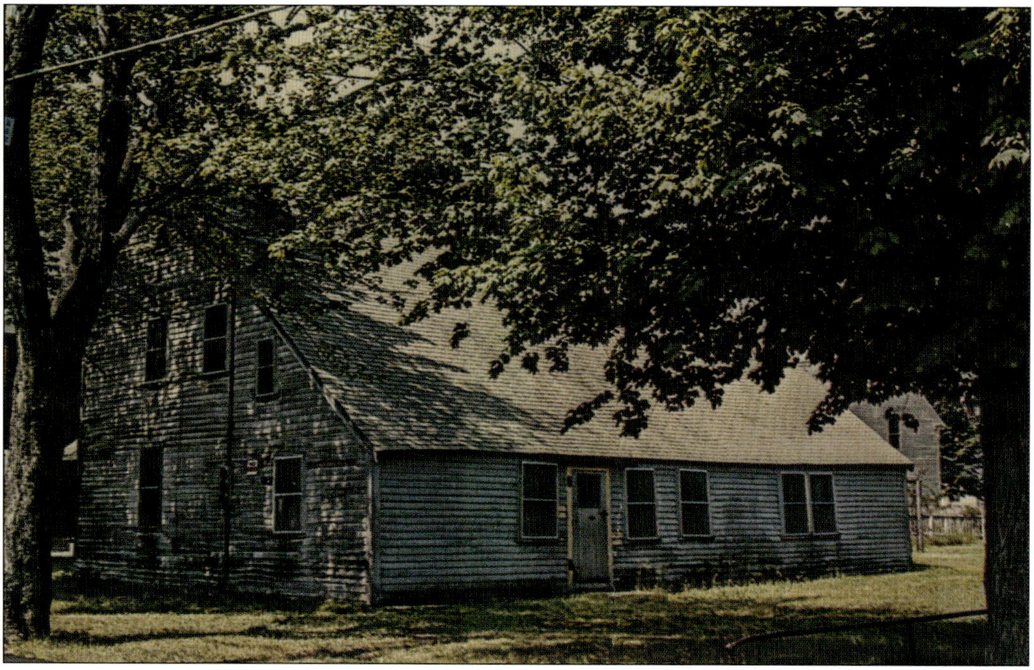

The Osgood House is the oldest house in Amesbury, built before 1650. This is a photograph of the house before it was dismantled and moved to Dover, Massachusetts, in 1969. Below, they are in the process of dismantling the house so that it can be moved. (Above, courtesy of the Amesbury Public Library; below, courtesy of Dianne Cole.)

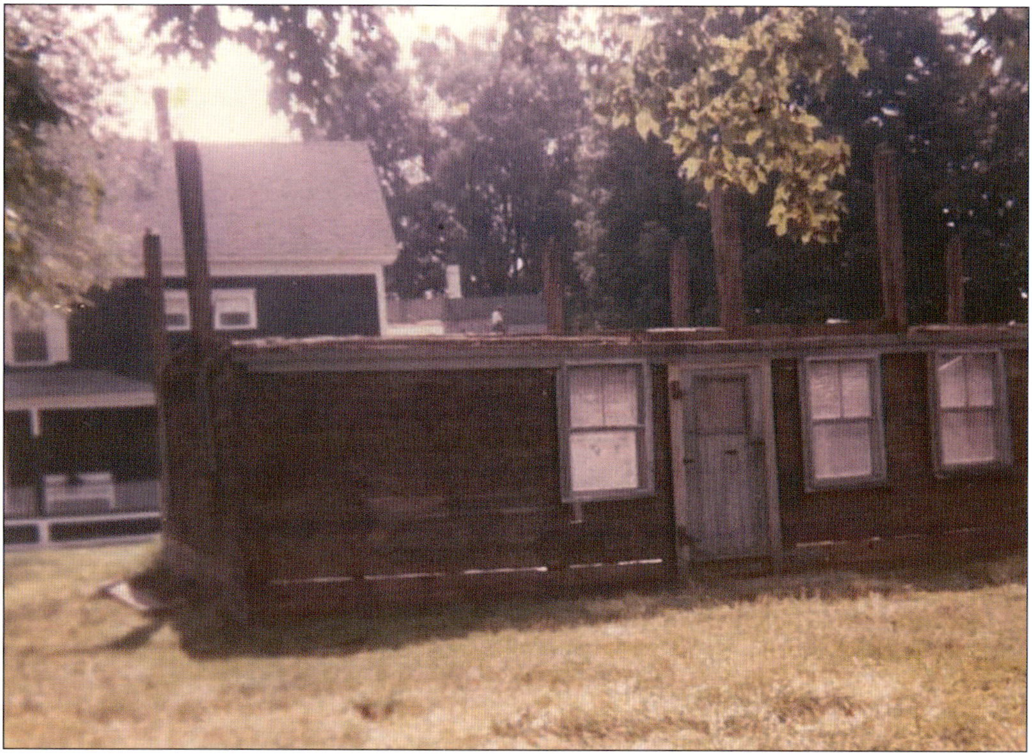

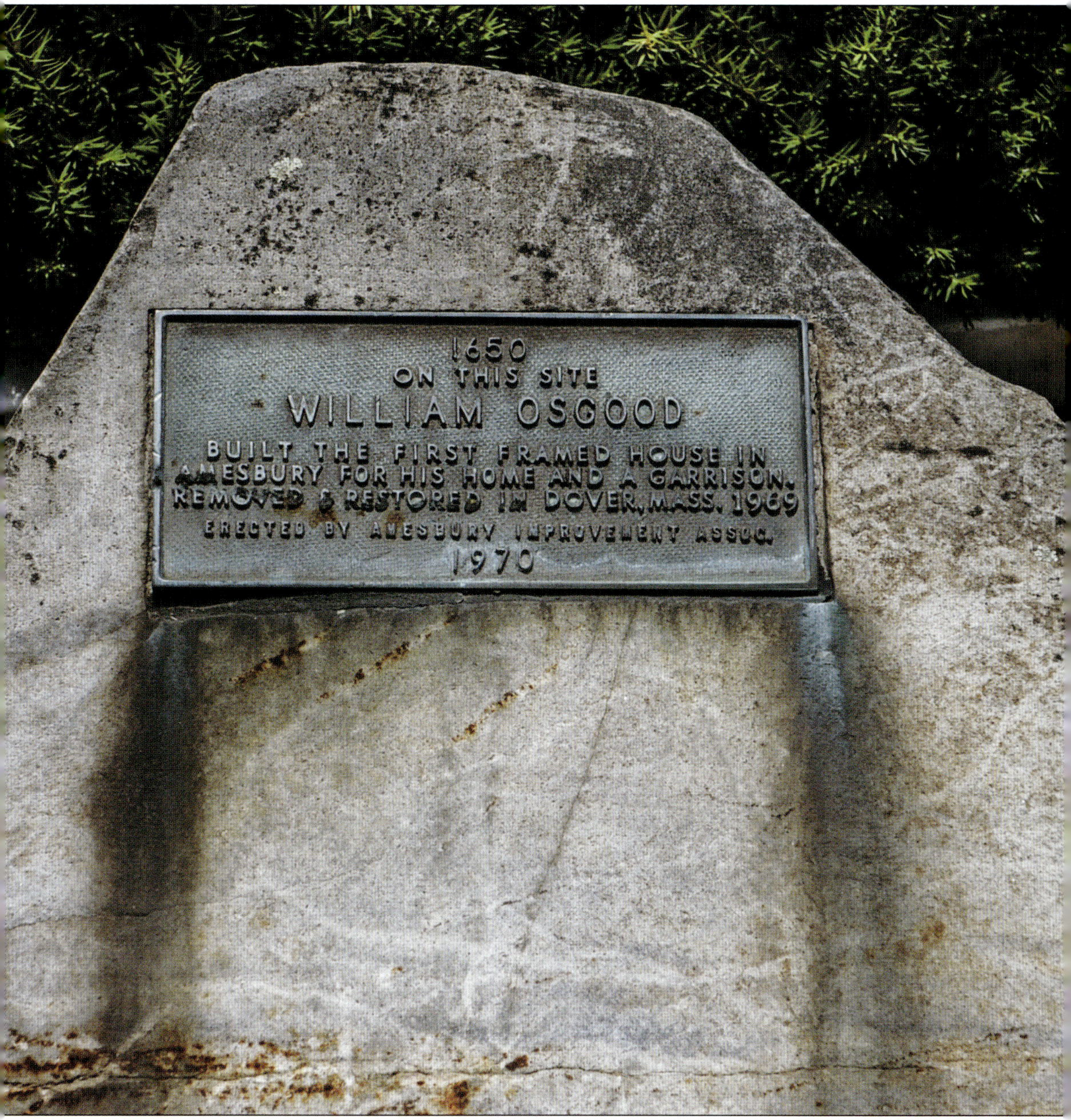

There is a monument on the corner of Congress and Colchester Streets in Amesbury that shows where the Osgood House once stood. This monument explains that this 1650 home was the first framed home in Amesbury. William Osgood also used it for a garrison. The house was moved in 1969 to Dover, Massachusetts. In 1970, the Amesbury Improvement Association created this historical marker. (Photograph by Joey Walker.)

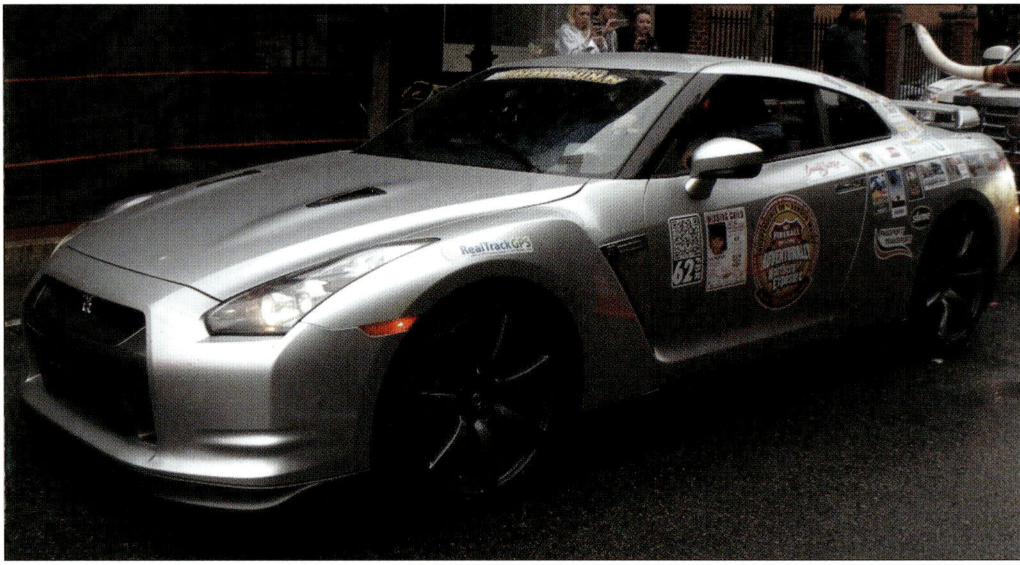

In 2012, Universal Studios' Fireball Run stopped in Amesbury as part of its 40-team amazing race. The race started in Ohio and ended in Bangor, Maine. Amesbury was the only city in Massachusetts on the stop route. The race is eight days and covers 2,500 miles. The race is filmed as part of the Race to Recovery of America's Missing Children. Each team is assigned a child from their region that is missing. Flyers and posters are passed out along the route. Through their efforts, 38 children have been found to date. Amesbury will have two participants in the race in 2016 and will be the finish line of the race. Bart Bailey and Ozzie Morrill will be taking the 1911 Bailey Electric Car via flatbed truck in the race. (Both, photograph by the author.)

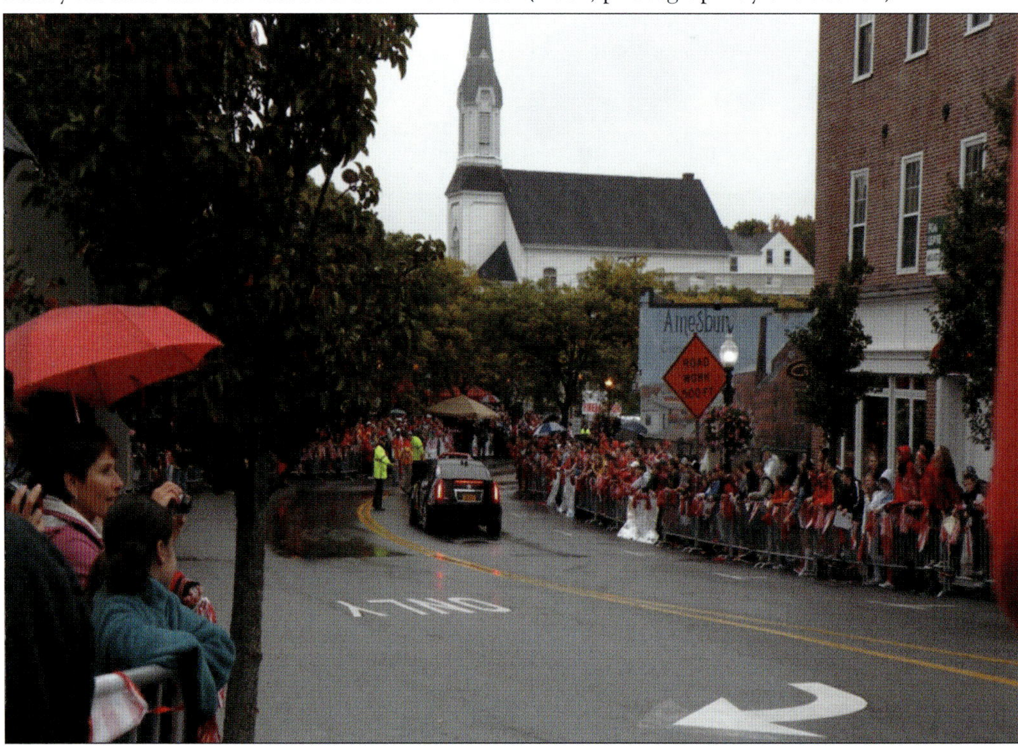

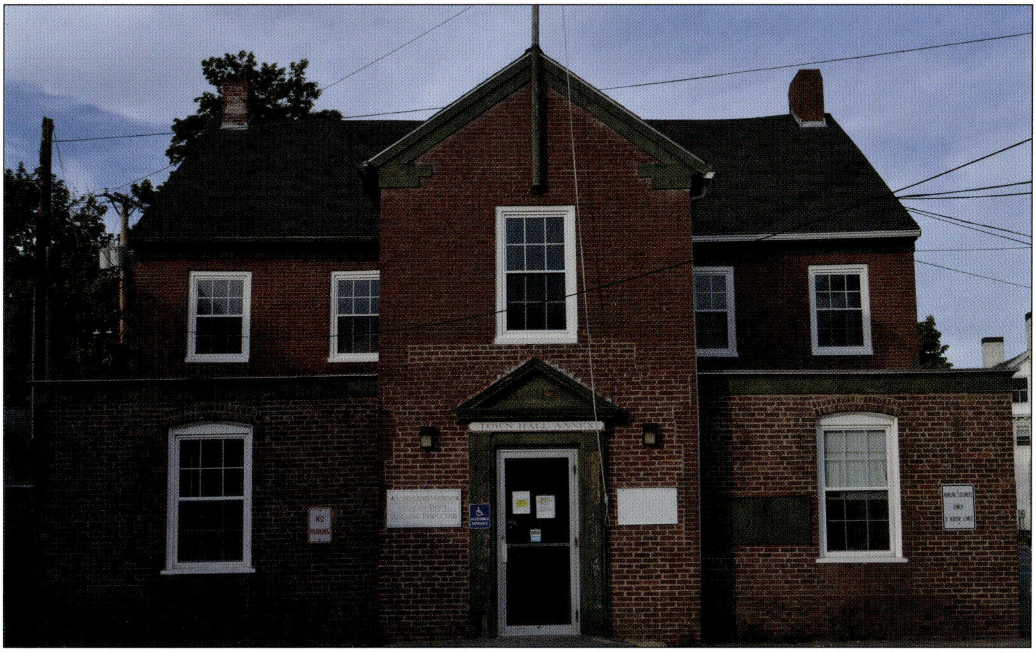

The annex building was one of the earlier schoolhouses. It was part of the Mills School District in the early 19th century. In 1889, the building was used by the Atlantic Hose Company, which was part of the fire department. In 1938, it was renovated by the WPA to be used as the school administration offices. In 2014, it was torn down to make room for the fire department's expansion. (Both, photograph by Joey Walker, courtesy of the Amesbury Public Library.)

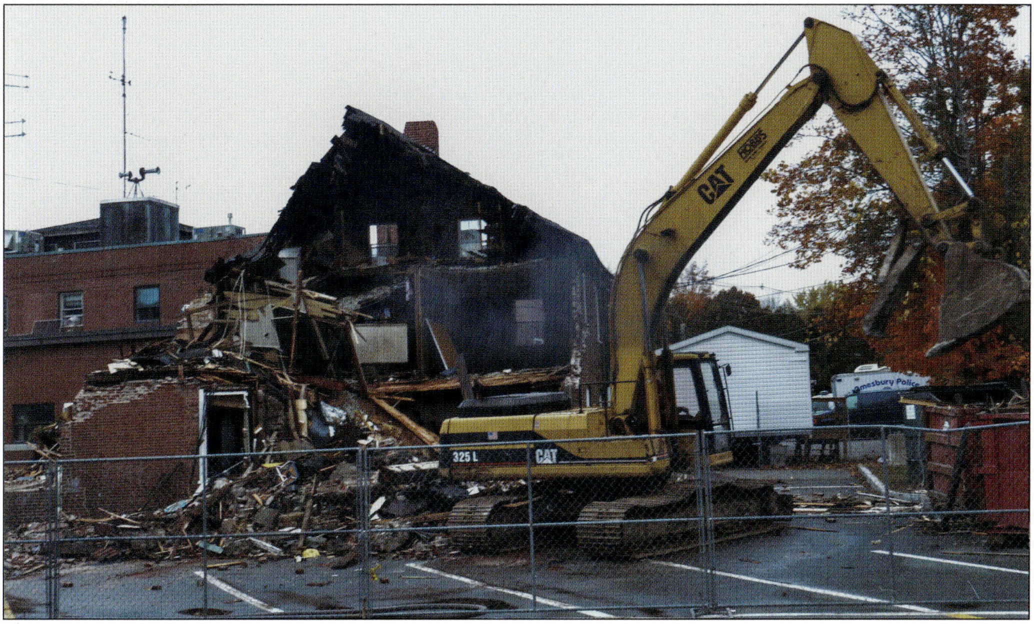

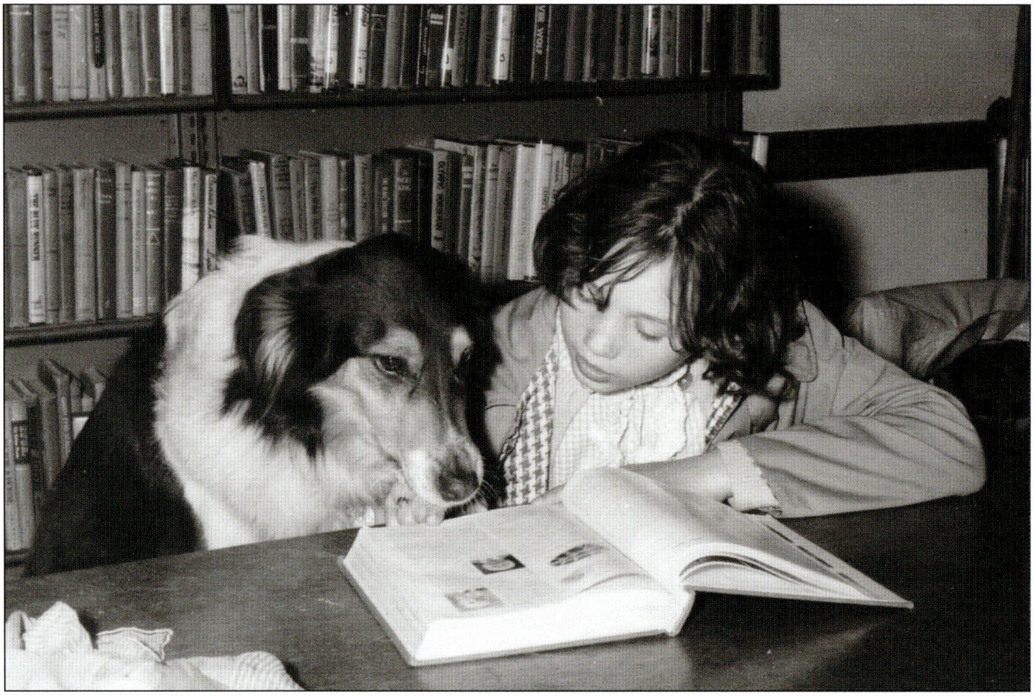

In 2015, libraries offer programs reading to service dogs to encourage and promote children reading. This unidentified young girl is on the cutting edge in this 1960 photograph. She is reading to her dog in the library. (Courtesy of the Amesbury Public Library.)

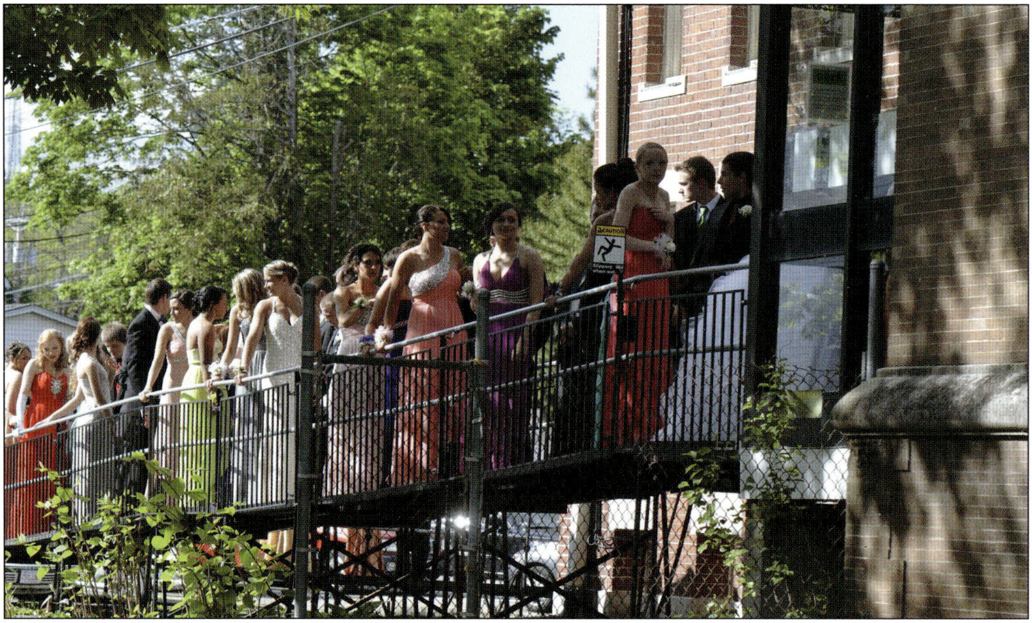

Since 2002, the Amesbury Public Library has been host to the Amesbury High School Junior Promenade. Volunteers decorate the front of the library and also the gazebo. Above, in 2013, participants line up in the library and proceed down the front steps to hundreds of spectators taking photographs. (Photograph by Joey Walker.)

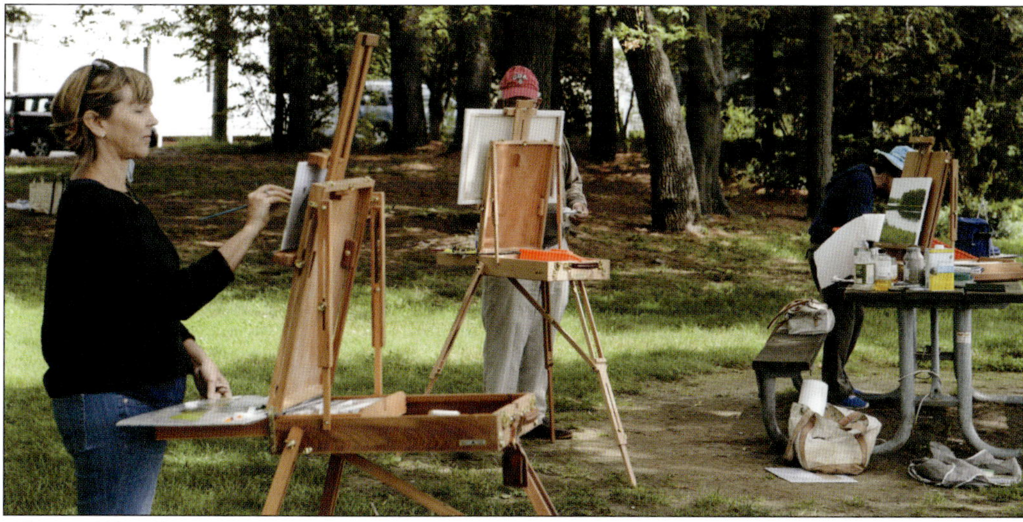

Alan Bull has his painting class at Alliance Park on Saturday mornings. From left to right, Tami Amoroso, Ledge Mitchell, and Barbara Gordon are working on their paintings of the scenery around the Merrimack River and Point Shore. (Photograph by Joey Walker.)

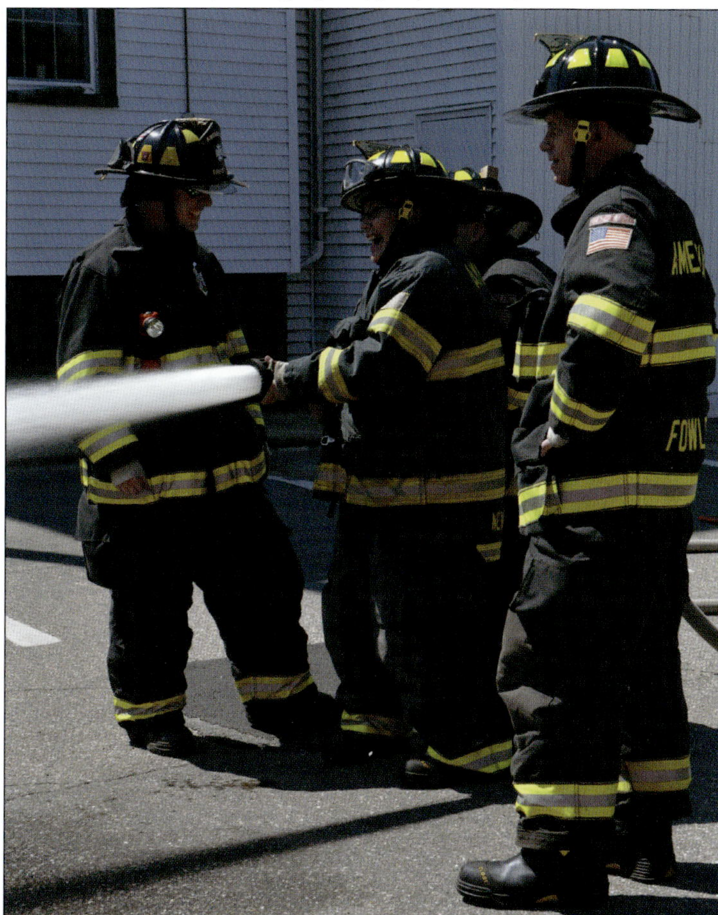

Councilwoman Anne Ferguson and then mayor Thatcher Kezer take part in the fire department's fire operations to give members of the community an idea of what it is like to be a firefighter. (Photograph by Joey Walker.)

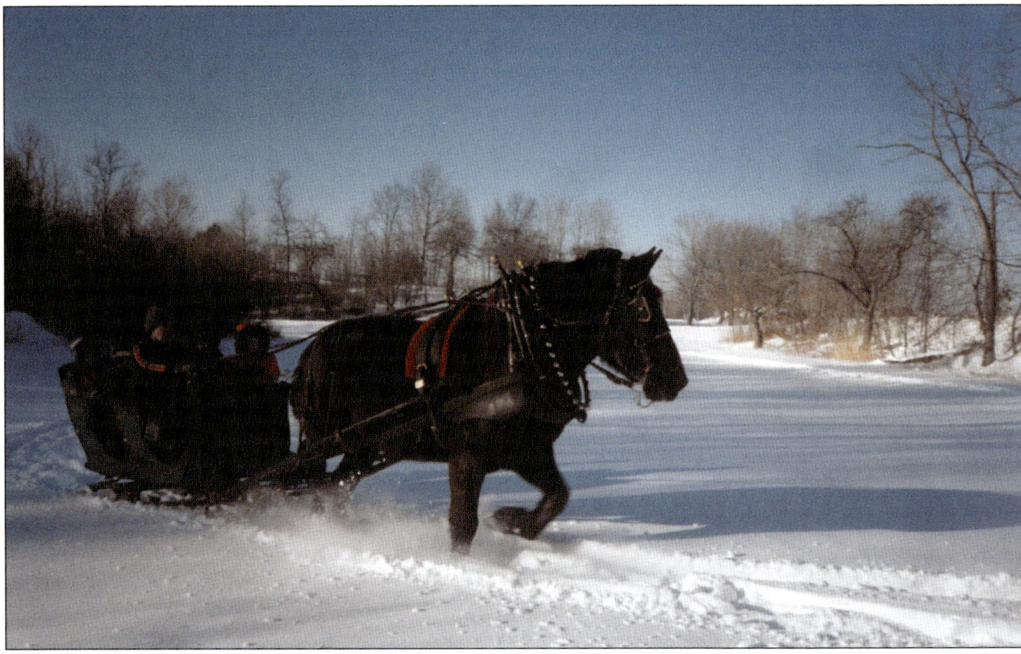

On this cold January day in 1991, Malcolm Odell takes his children out for a sleigh ride in this winter wonderland at Woodsom Farm. (Courtesy of the Amesbury Carriage Museum.)

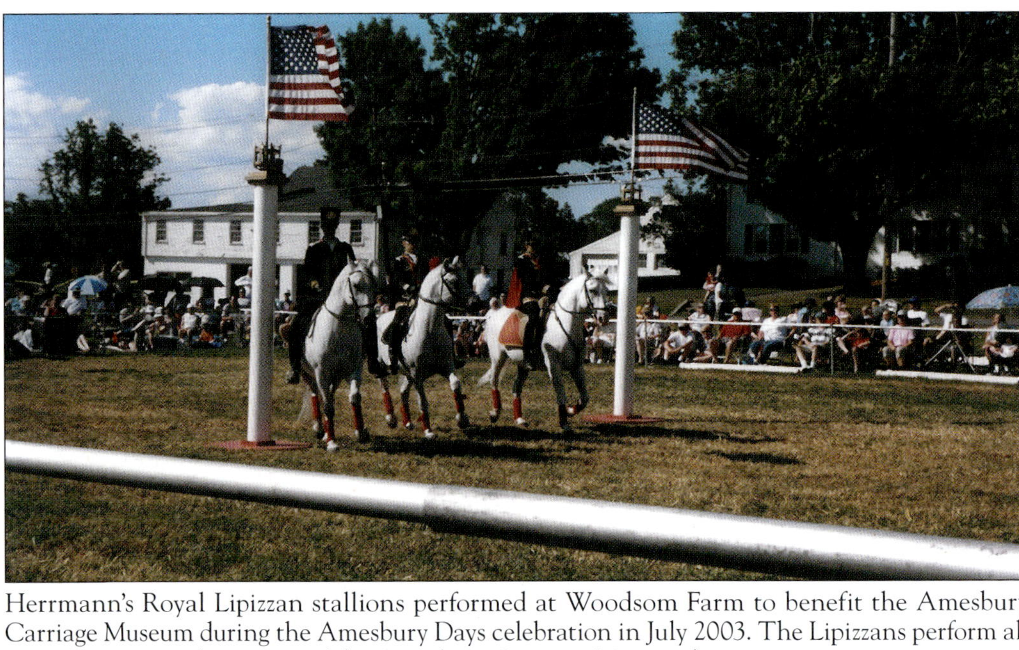

Herrmann's Royal Lipizzan stallions performed at Woodsom Farm to benefit the Amesbury Carriage Museum during the Amesbury Days celebration in July 2003. The Lipizzans perform all over the country. (Courtesy of the Amesbury Carriage Museum.)

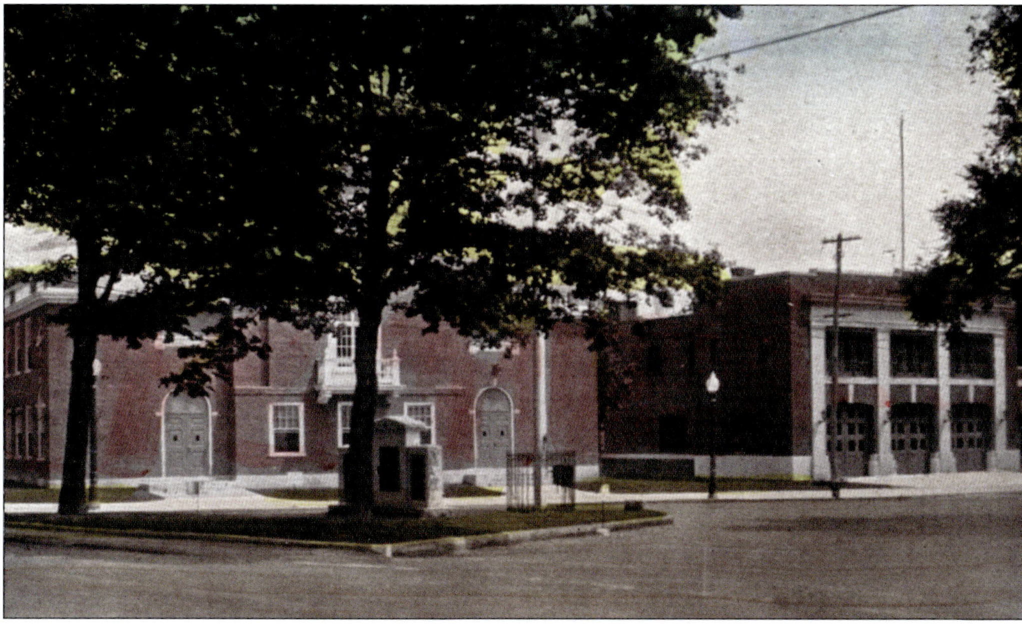

The Amesbury Police Station is on the corner of Friend and School Streets. It was built in 1930. At one time it was the Amesbury District Court. (Courtesy of the Amesbury Public Library.)

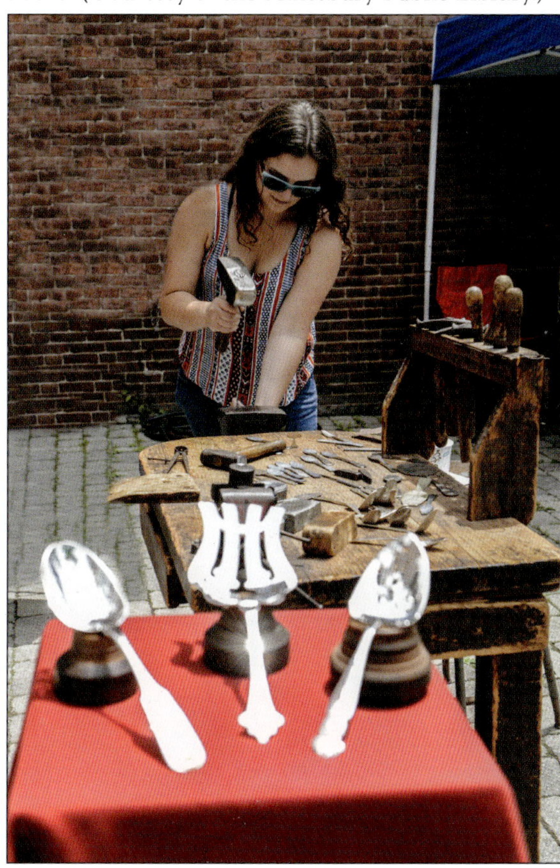

Chloe Darke is a silversmith at Old Newbury Crafters in downtown Amesbury. All of its products are made by hand, starting with a block of silver. The silver starts taking shape at the anvil. There is no cutting. The five-pound hammer is being forged on the polished surface of the anvil. Darke is demonstrating silverware making in 2015. Old Newbury Crafters are proud to make American-made products. (Photograph by Joey Walker.)

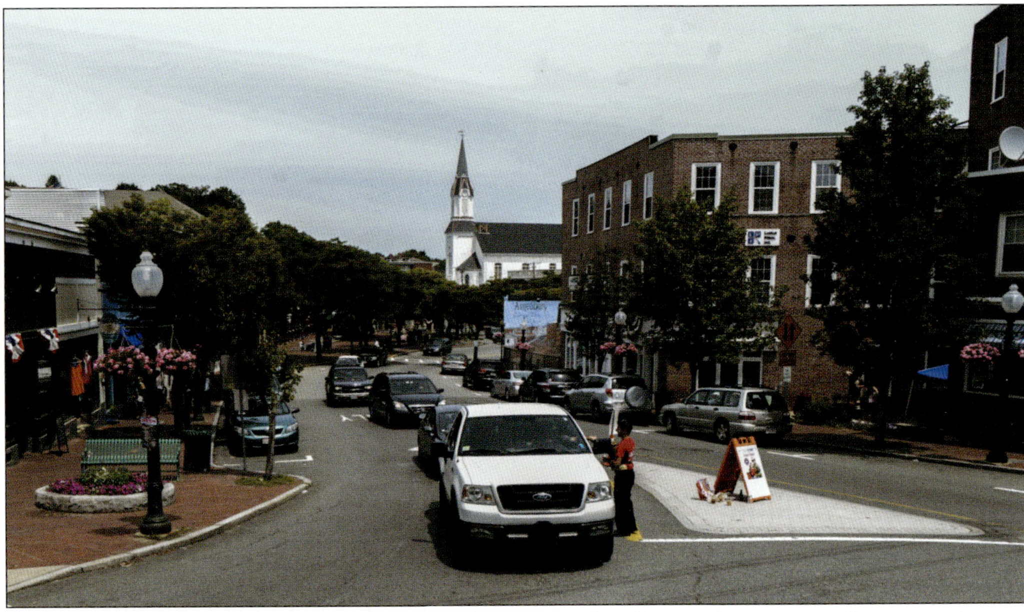

Downtown Amesbury is pictured here on a busy Saturday during the summer. Stores are having their sidewalk sales, and people are demonstrating their crafts. Firemen are collecting for an organization, and residents are happy to stop and help. Market Street Baptist Church is looking good with its repaired steeple. (Photograph by Joey Walker.)

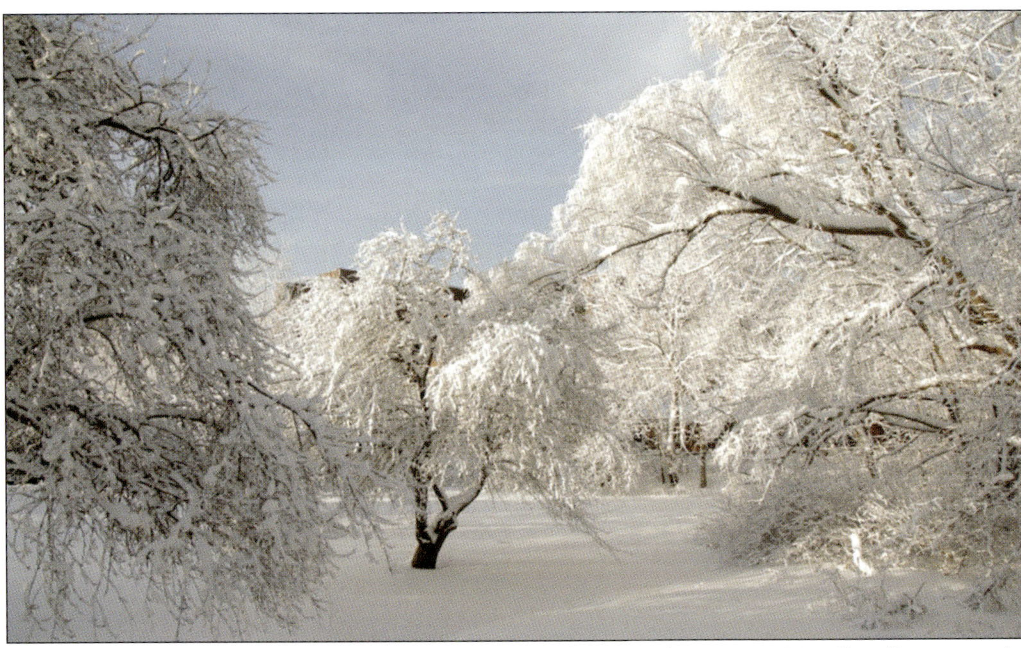

The blizzard of 2015 dropped 30 inches of snow in the Amesbury area. Unofficially, it was the biggest recorded snowfall in the area since the blizzard of 1978. Businesses and schools were closed, as Department of Public Works employees worked night and day to dig the city out. Residents were grateful for all of their hard work. (Photograph by the author.)

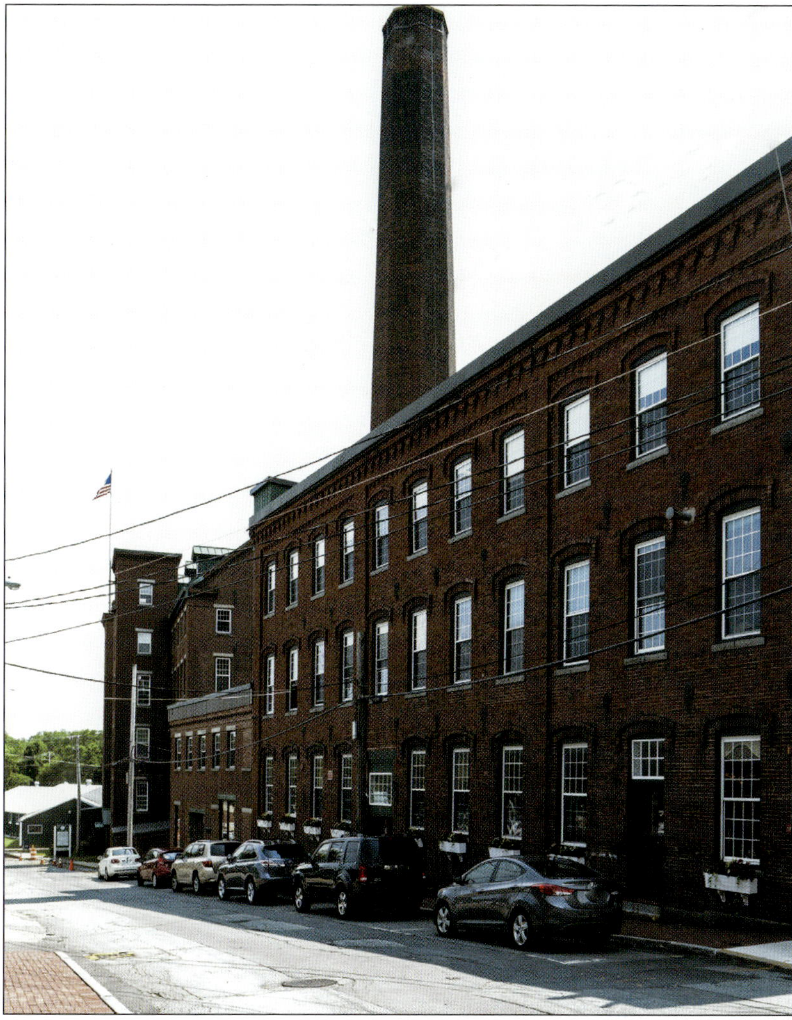

This mill building houses the Artists' Muse, where local artists, jewelers, and photographers can sell their items. The future home of the carriage museum, the chamber of commerce, and a visitors' center, Heritage Park will be just below the mill building. (Photograph by Joey Walker.)

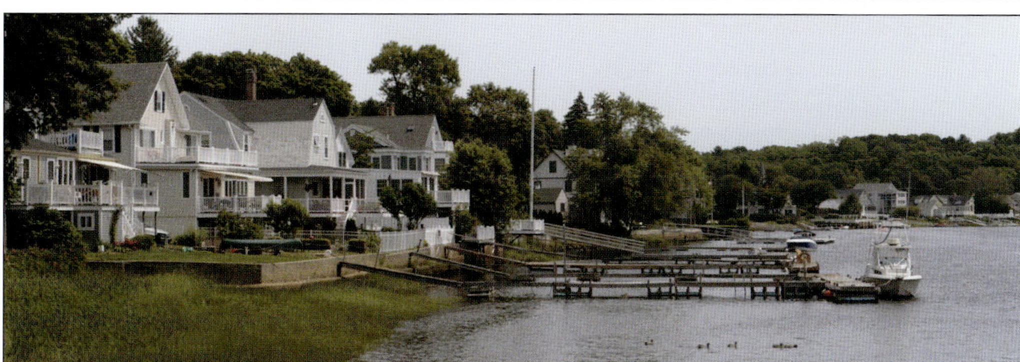

Point Shore runs along the Merrimack River going toward Newburyport. Alliance Park, Union Congregational Church, and Lowell's Boat Shop call Point Shore home. People that live along the Merrimack have beautiful views of the river and the birds that make their home there. As one drives along, private docks with boats tied up can be seen. Poet Robert Frost called Point Shore his summer home. (Photograph by the author.)

Pleasant Valley Road is a narrow two-lane road that runs along the Merrimack River into the town of Merrimac, which used to be West Amesbury. There is limited access to the river, but some houses have docks. Much of the farmland is now developed into housing and condominiums. (Photograph by Joey Walker.)

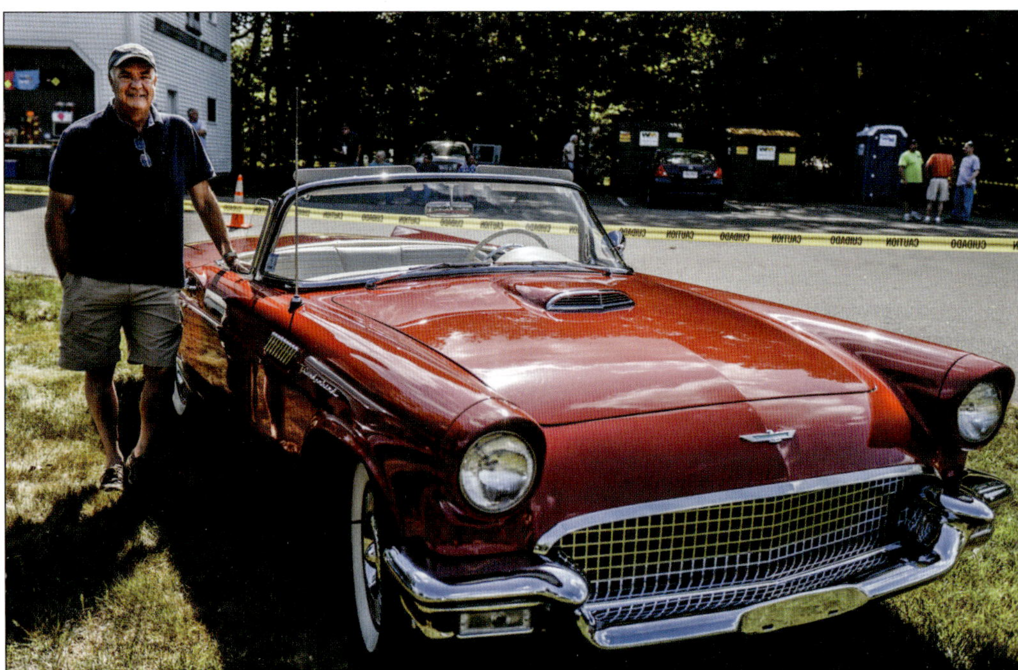

Ken Gray was elected mayor in 2013. One of his passions is his 1957 Ford Thunderbird named Elizabeth. One can see Mayor Gray some weekend mornings down at Alliance Park polishing his car, at the Amesbury Days' car show, and at National Night Out activities. (Photograph by Joey Walker.)

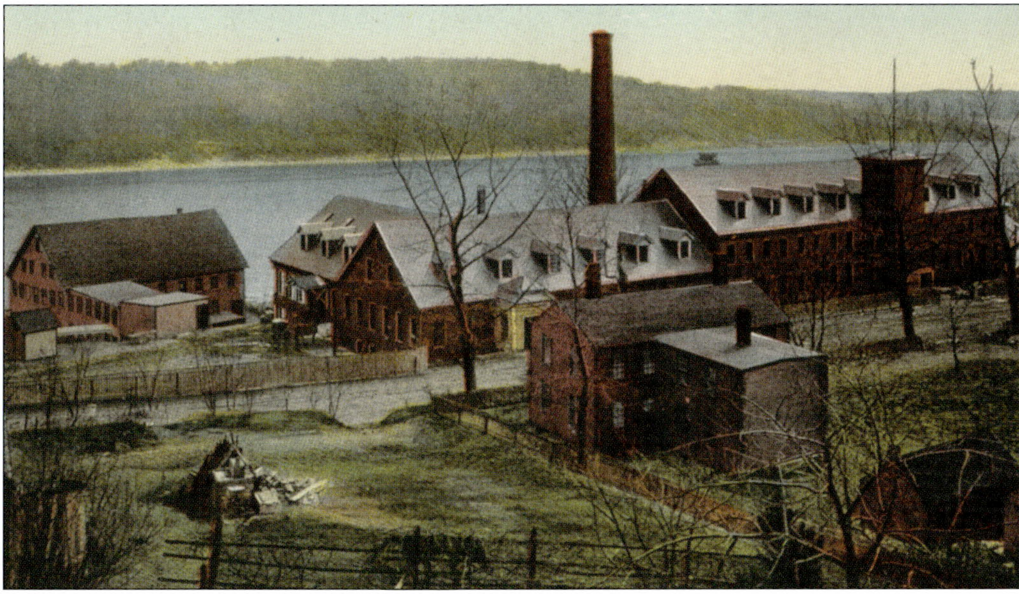

The Merrimac Hat Company, formed by Abner Bailey, was in business from 1856 until 1970. The hats were made for men and women and shipped all over the country. The doors closed in 1970. It is now known as Hatter's Point Condominiums, located right along the Merrimack River, for people aged 55 and over. (Both, photograph by Joey Walker; courtesy of the Amesbury Public Library.)

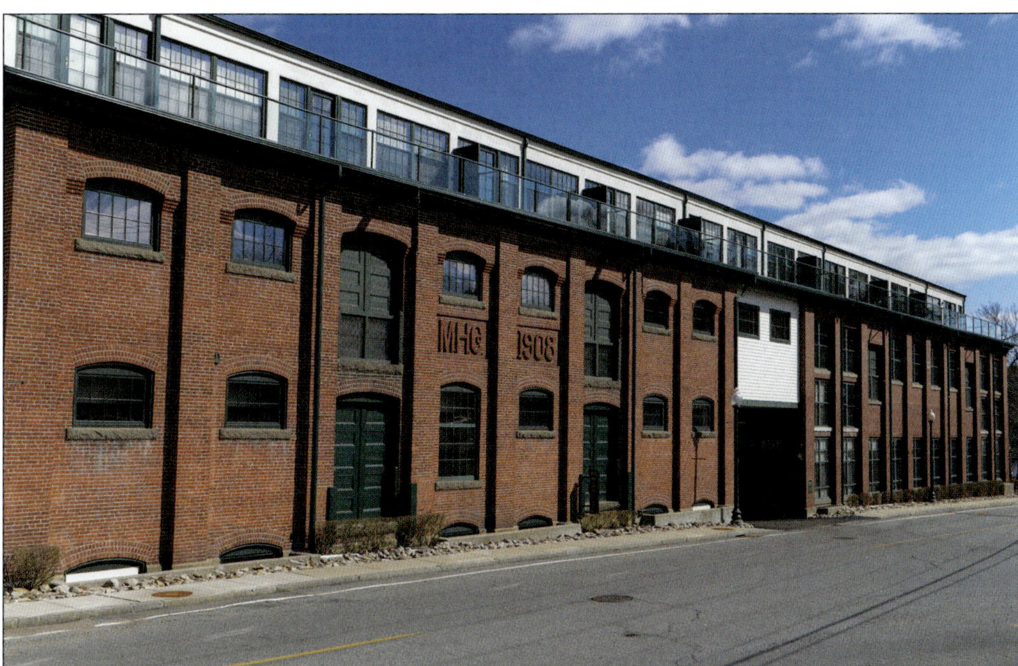

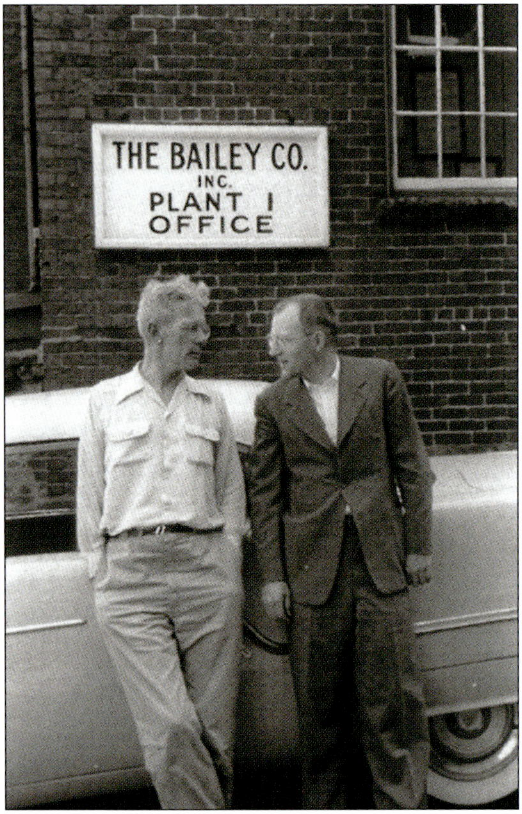

Edwin Bailey (left) and William Pottle (right) stop in front of Bailey Plant 1 in late 1950s talking business. The Baileys were prominent in town, building carriages and automobiles. In the 1970s, they moved their company to Seabrook, New Hampshire. (Courtesy of the Amesbury Public Library.)

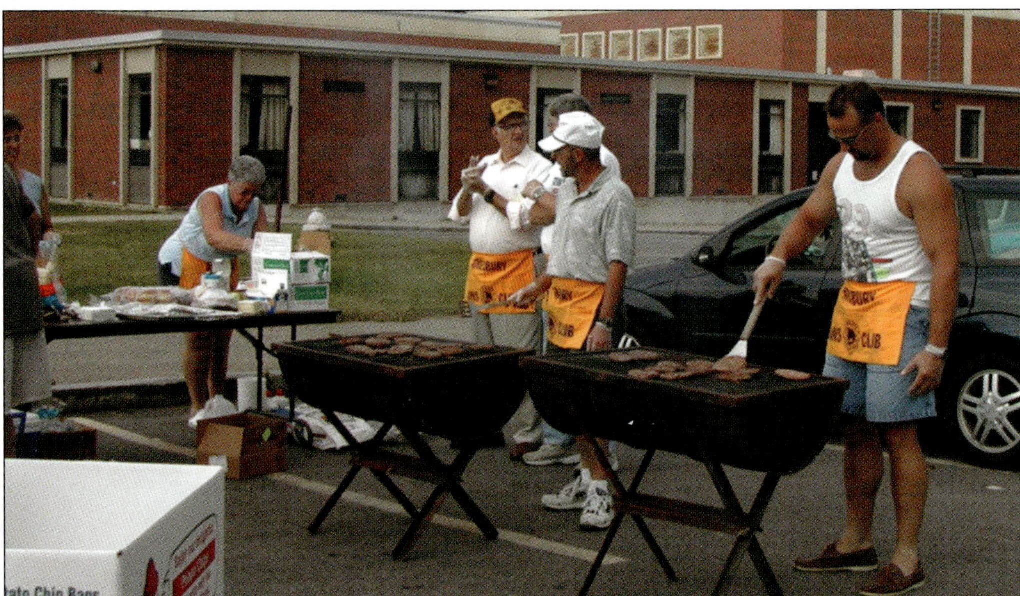

The Lions Club does a lot for Amesbury. They provide the eye mobile, vision assistance, hearing assistance, and scholarships. Here, from left to right, Joni Baptiste, Connie Pare, Aurel LeBlanc, Randy Baptiste, Peter Grenier, and Matt Sherrill are flipping burgers at a town event at Amesbury High School. (Photograph by the author.)

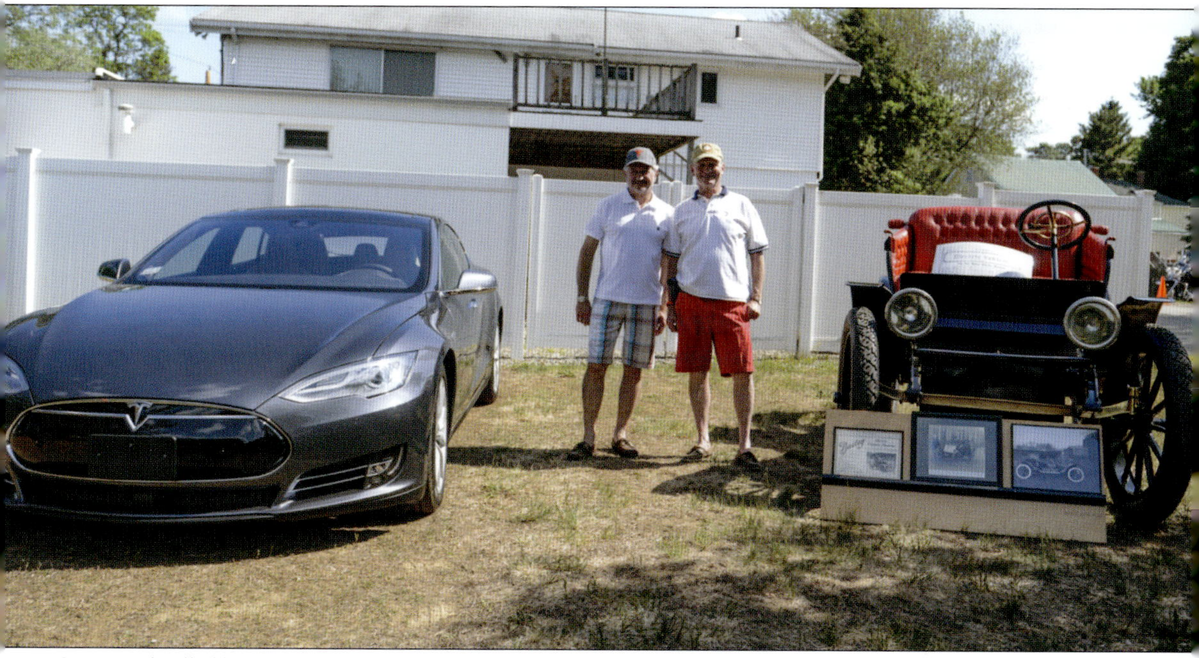

Greg Jardis (left) owner of Amesbury Industrial, is pictured here with his 2015 Tesla electric car, which can go 240 miles on a charge. Bart Bailey (right) of B&B Security Systems is pictured with the Electric Victoria Phaeton that was built by his family, the S.R. Bailey Company, in 1911 and can go 100 miles on a charge. The S.R. Bailey Company had the right idea when they built the first model in 1911. The Victoria Phaeton will be part of the Fireball Run in 2016. It will be glassed in on a flatbed truck going along the route, bringing awareness to missing children. Amesbury has added charging stations in the lower millyard for people to charge their electric cars while they shop downtown. (Photograph by Joey Walker.)

INDEX